B-26 Marauder

Written by Hans-Heiri Stapfer

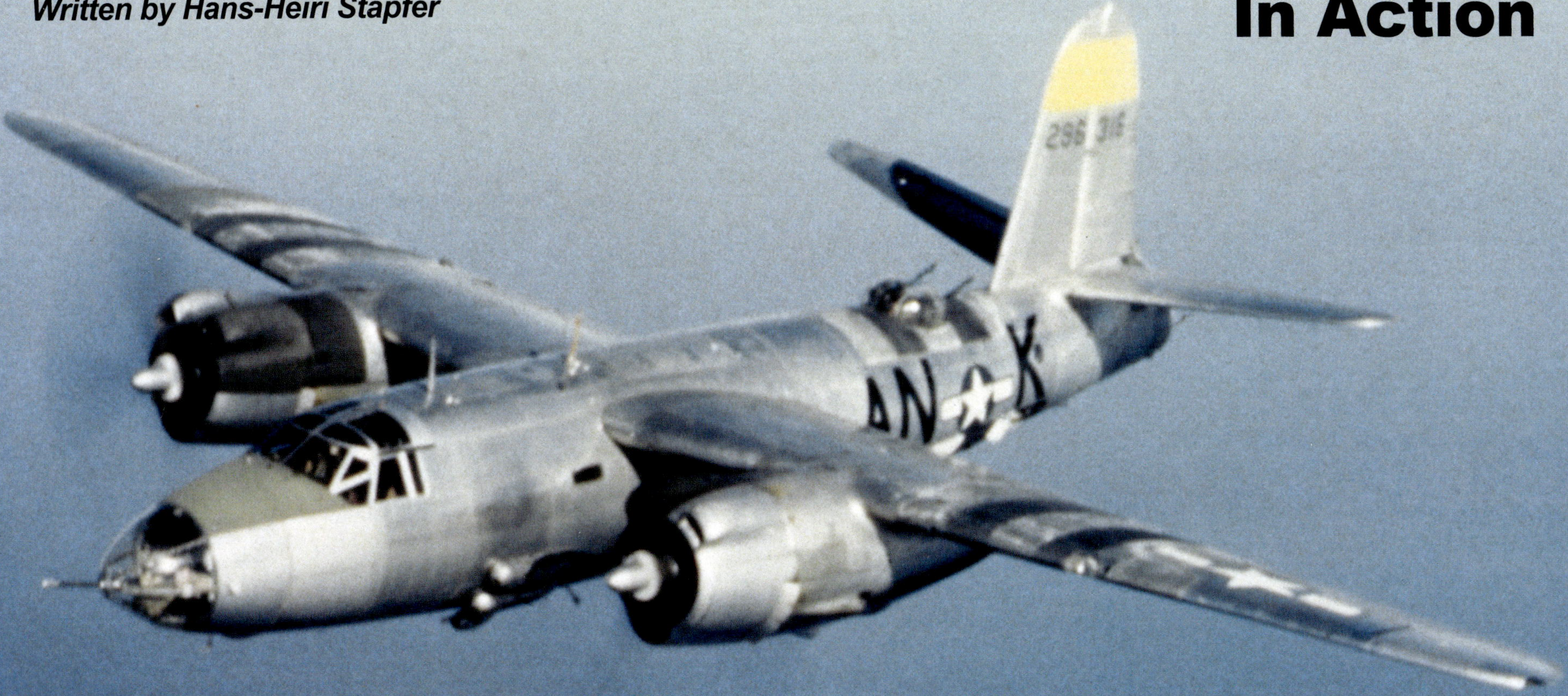

In Action

Color Art by Don Greer

Line Illustrations by Ike Anderson

(Front Cover) Led by B-26 C-45-MO "Yellow 80," veteran B-26 B-10-MA "Yellow 93" and a new, unnumbered B-26 G-5-MA drop their loads. The shark mouth was the squadron insignia of the 444th Bomb Squadron of the 320th Bomb Group. This unit belonged to the 42nd Bomb Wing, Twelfth Air Force, Mediterranean Theater of Operations.

(Back Cover) Led by *Flak Bait,* these 322nd Bomb Group Marauders warm up their engines at A-89 Le Culot air base in Belgium on 24 April 1945, the last mission for *Flak Bait.* This B-26 B-25-MA (41-31773) flew more missions than any other Allied bomber in World War II: 202 missions with the 322nd Bomb Group.

About the In Action® Series

In Action® books, despite the title of the genre, are books that trace the development of a single type of aircraft, armored vehicle, or ship from prototype to the final production variant. Experimental or "one-off" variants can also be included. Our first *In Action®* book was printed in 1971.

ISBN 978-0-89747-549-5

Copyright 2015, 2008 Squadron/Signal Publications
1115 Crowley Drive, Carrollton, TX 75006-1312 U.S.A.

All rights reserved. No part of this publication may be reproduced, stored in a retrieval system, or transmitted in any form by means electrical, mechanical, or otherwise, without written permission of the publisher.

Military/Combat Photographs and Snapshots

If you have any photos of aircraft, armor, soldiers, or ships of any nation, particularly wartime snapshots, why not share them with us and help make Squadron/Signal's books all the more interesting and complete in the future? Any photograph sent to us will be copied and returned. Electronic images are preferred. The donor will be fully credited for any photos used. Please send them to:

Squadron/Signal Publications
1115 Crowley Drive
Carrollton, TX 75006-1312 U.S.A.
www.SquadronSignalPublications.com

(Title Page) This B-26 F-1-MA (42-96316) AN-K of the 386th Bomb Group 553rd Bomb Squadron crosses the English Channel *en route* to blast German strong points in occupied France shortly after the Allied invasion at Normandy had unfolded on 6 June 1944. (John H. Meyers)

Acknowledgments

Albert F. Simpson Historical Research Center, Steve Birdsall, Eddie J. Creek, Michel Cristescu, Alan Crouchman, Bernhard Ecklin, The Glenn L. Martin Maryland Aviation Museum (GLMMAM), Kerstin Gutbrod, Jack K. Havener, Harry Holmes, Karl Kössler, Martin Kyburz, Lockheed Martin, John H. Meyers, Alain Pelletier, G.W. Prinsloo, Royal Air Force Museum, South African Department of Defence, Smithsonian Institution, Jay P. Spenser, John Stanaway, Victor C. Tannehill and the U.S. Navy. Special thanks go to the Glenn L. Martin Maryland Aviation Museum at Baltimore (www.marylandaviationmuseum.org) and the B-26 Marauder Historical Society (www.b-26mhs.org).

B-26 Marauders belonging to the 386th Bomb Group head to the Normandy beachheads in France on 6 June 1944. Marauders, all wearing the distinctive black-and-white D-Day stripes on their wings and rear fuselages, were among the very first U.S. aircraft over the beachheads that day, as the Allied invasion of Nazi-occupied Europe unfolded. The 386th Bomb Group performed an astonishing total of four missions on 6 June 1944, attacking costal guns at St. Martin de Varreville, la Madeleine, les Dunes de Varreville, and Houlgate. The B-26s dropped their bomb loads from about 3,500 feet. The Marauder in the foreground is *Mr. Five by Five,* a B-26 B-15-MA (41-31612) assigned to the 555th Bomb Squadron, 386th Bomb Group, with the unit marking YA-Z. Below, in the English Channel, are landing craft headed for the action in Normandy. (Harry Holmes)

Introduction

Probably no other aircraft type in the inventory of the United States Army Air Force (USAAF) can rival the reputation of the Martin B-26 Marauder. *Flak Bait* was the only American bomber that accomplished more than 200 missions during World War II. In addition, Martin's medium bomber had a loss rate of less than 1 percent – the lowest loss rate of any American bomber operated during the war. Over 60 percent of the Marauders that started bombing operations from English bases during the summer of 1943 were still operational a year later. Among B-17 and B-24 units this figure was less than 2 percent.

On the other hand, the B-26 acquired quite a reputation as a widow maker, a reputation that was never fully corrected during its operational career and that was the main reason that most B-26s were scrapped shortly after the end of hostilities. A total of 129,943 Marauder sorties over Europe were recorded by the USAAF, this at the cost of 911 B-26s lost in combat. The Marauders belonging to the 9th and 12th Air Force dropped a total of 169,382 tons of bombs, mainly on tactical targets, such as bridges, enemy strong points, and marshalling yards, but also on V1 flying bomb sites in Northern France. Between November 1940 and March 1945, a total of 5,266 B-26s were built. Many senior pilots of the 22nd Bomb Group in Australia – the outfit that pioneered the Marauder – recalled the B-26 as "the best damn airplane the Air Force ever had." And there is nothing more to add.

On 11 March 1939, the Material Division at Wright Field, Ohio, issued Circular Proposal 39-640 for a medium bomber. The Army Air Force requirements called for the same bomb load as on the heavy Boeing B-17 Flying Fortress four-engine bomber and a top speed of 300 miles per hour. The Glenn L. Martin Company in Baltimore developed Model 179 at its Middle River plant. The Middle River plant was founded by Glenn Luther Martin, an old-time flyer but no engineer and an extremely autocratic and arbitrary individual. No fewer than 15 different internal design concepts were compared. Three different engines – the Wright R-2600 and R-3350 as well the Pratt & Whitney R-2800 – were considered. One of the early proposals also included a two-tail configuration.

The final Martin proposal that was submitted to the Army Air Force included the Pratt & Whitney R-2800 powerplant and a wing of only 605 square feet. The 28-year-old chief designer, Peyton Marshall Magruder, had finally settled on the single vertical tail configuration. Besides Martin, North American, Douglas, and Stearman also submitted proposals. The Army Air Force selected Model 179 as its new medium bomber on 5 July 1939, less than two months before the outbreak of World War II. Contract AC-13243, with a value of $15,815,000, called for 201 B-26 aircraft, the largest order ever placed by the Army Air Force, which then issued an additional order for another 139 aircraft on 16 September 1939. The original designation, Martin Model 179, was changed to B-26. The name "Marauder" became official some time later, in October 1941, on British initiative.

The B-26 design was well ahead of its time. It was the first combat aircraft in which the designers used butted seams for the skin covering as opposed to the conventional lapped seams. This feature enhanced the flow of air over the streamlined torpedo-like fuselage and increased the aircraft's speed. The Marauder was also the first aircraft to be equipped with a power-operated gun turret. The electrically operated 250 CE turret with two Browning M-2 0.50-caliber machine guns was a Martin innovation. The turret was so successful that a total of 56,000 units were built and served in 27 different types of aircraft. The B-26 also became the first bomber with rubber self-sealing fuel tanks and an all-electrical bomb release mechanism installed as regular equipment. The Marauder was the first aircraft to mount the giant 18-cylinder Pratt & Whitney R-2800-5. The two-row radial engine offered an output of 1,850 h.p. at take off. Another "first" was accomplished with the choice of the propeller: The B-26 became the first bomber to be equipped with four-blade propellers, driven by two Curtis electrically controlled airscrews. Martin made use of plastic materials as metal substitutes on a grand scale. A further Martin innovation was the first all-Plexiglas nose introduced on an American bomber. This nose offered better visibility than the "greenhouse" noses on the B-17 Flying Fortress and the North American B-25 Mitchell.

The semi-monocoque aluminum alloy fuselage was fabricated in three sections. The fuselage was circular in cross section except for the small flat areas behind the cockpit side windows. The structure had four main longerons, transverse circular frames, and longitudinal stringers covered by an alloy skin. The mid-section with the bomb bays was built integrally with the wing section. The primary wing structure was box type, formed by two tension field-web beams and top and bottom thick-gauge skin reinforced by nut section members to give a torsionally rigid structure. Continuous hinges attaching the leading edge to the primary structure facilitated maintenance. The retractable tricycle-landing gear was hydraulically actuated, the nose wheel pivoting 90 degrees to retract into the nose section, and the main wheels folding back into the engine nacelles. The tail fins were of box, smooth stressed skin cantilever structure consisting of two tension field type beams with sheet metal ribs. The elevators were covered by metal, but the rudder was fabric covered. The B-26 was designed for rapid production. Spot welding and large aluminum forging replaced a number of riveted parts. The Glenn L. Martin Company purchased stretch presses of the sort used in automobile factories to reduce the amount of drop-hammer work on complex skin fairing.

No fewer than 15 different internal design concepts were compared on the Model 179 by the Glenn L. Martin Company. Initially a two-tail configuration was considered for the Model 179, which subsequently emerged as the B-26 Marauder. This mock up with a twin tail configuration was demonstrated on 3 July 1939. Chief designer Peyton Marshall Magruder finally decided in favor of the single vertical tail configuration. (GLMMAM)

The First B-26

An Army Air Corps board had the opportunity to inspect a mock up of the B-26 in November 1939, 12 months before the plane would take to the air for the first time. There was no prototype selected and the first B-26 built also became the first production aircraft for the Army Air Force. Compared with the original Army Air Force specification, the actual empty weight of 21,375 pounds was 2,155 pounds over the requested weight. After a number of taxi tests, the first B-26 (40-1361) took off from the Glenn L. Martin factory field at Middle River at Baltimore on 25 November 1940. Chief Engineer William K. Ebel, then 41 years old, took the aircraft for its maiden flight, with Bob Fenimore as co-pilot and Al Melewski as the flight engineer. The only shortcoming detected by the crew was a slight aerodynamic overbalance in the rudder. The factory flight test program revealed a top speed of 315 miles per hour at 15,000 feet.

The B-26 was as speedy as a fighter, but carried roughly the same bomb load as a B-17 Flying Fortress. The aircraft's short wingspan of only 65 feet reduced drag and yielded greater speed. On the down side, it also gave the plane a high landing speed of 130 miles per hour that necessitated a skilled pilot and full attention during the landing procedure. The contemporary North American NA-40 – the prototype of the B-25 Mitchell – had a span of 66 feet and a top speed of 285 miles per hour. No armament was carried on the first B-26 during factory flight testing, but defensive armament on subsequent production examples augmented the two 0.50-caliber machine guns in the top turret with a flexible Browning M-2 0.30-caliber in the nose plus a Browning of the same caliber in the ventral position and another in the tail.

After some extensive prototype testing at the factory, the first B-26 was allocated to Laughlin Field in Del Rio, Texas, where the bomber served as transition trainer. At that time the B-26 had received the standard Army Air Force camouflage of dark olive drab on the upper and neutral gray on the lower surfaces. During the course of operation at Laughlin, the plane received the nickname *Gran Pappy*. Eventually, the first B-26 was scrapped in February 1945. A unique feature of the first B-26 was the L-shaped probe mounted on the starboard Pitot tube as well the static discharger mounted on the nose wheel strut. Both items were deleted from subsequent aircraft.

The sophisticated design of the B-26 had its price: the Martin bomber had a unit price of $79,602 and was $16,000 or 25 percent more expensive than the North American B-25 Mitchell. At the time production was launched at Middle River, a total of 38,900 man-hours were needed to complete a single Marauder, while the remarkable larger four-engine Boeing B-17 Flying Fortress rolled out after only 33,000 hours.

Before the first B-26 had even flown, the Army Air Force placed a further order for an additional 791 Marauders on 28 September 1940. These orders made an expansion of the existing facility necessary and a second production line was set up at the Middle River plant in Baltimore. Thousands of new workers migrated into the city, causing severe overcrowding. New housing projects sprang up around the Middle River plant: "Aero Aces" and "Victory Villa" boasted appropriate street names like Fuselage Avenue and Right and Left Wing Drives. Overcrowding was also relived by the recruitment of local woman and African Americans, hitherto excluded from production jobs at the Glenn L. Martin Company. At its peak in 1943, a total of 53,000 employees worked at Martin's Middle River plant.

A unique feature of the first B-26 (40-1361) ever built was the L-shaped probe mounted atop the starboard Pitot tube on the wing tip leading edge. This probe was deleted on all subsequent aircraft. After the factory testing had been terminated, the first Marauder had been camouflaged and served as a transition trainer at Laughlin Field at Del Rio in Texas. This B-26 was scrapped in February 1945. (GLMMAM)

No prototype of the Marauder was built. The B-26 (40-1361) was the first aircraft of an initial Army Air Corps order of 201 aircraft. The plane took off for the first time on 25 November 1940 from the Glenn L. Martin factory field at Middle River in Baltimore. The crew on its maiden flight consisted Chief Engineer William K. Ebel, co-pilot Bob Fenimore, and flight engineer Al Melewski. (GLMMAM)

Marauder Development

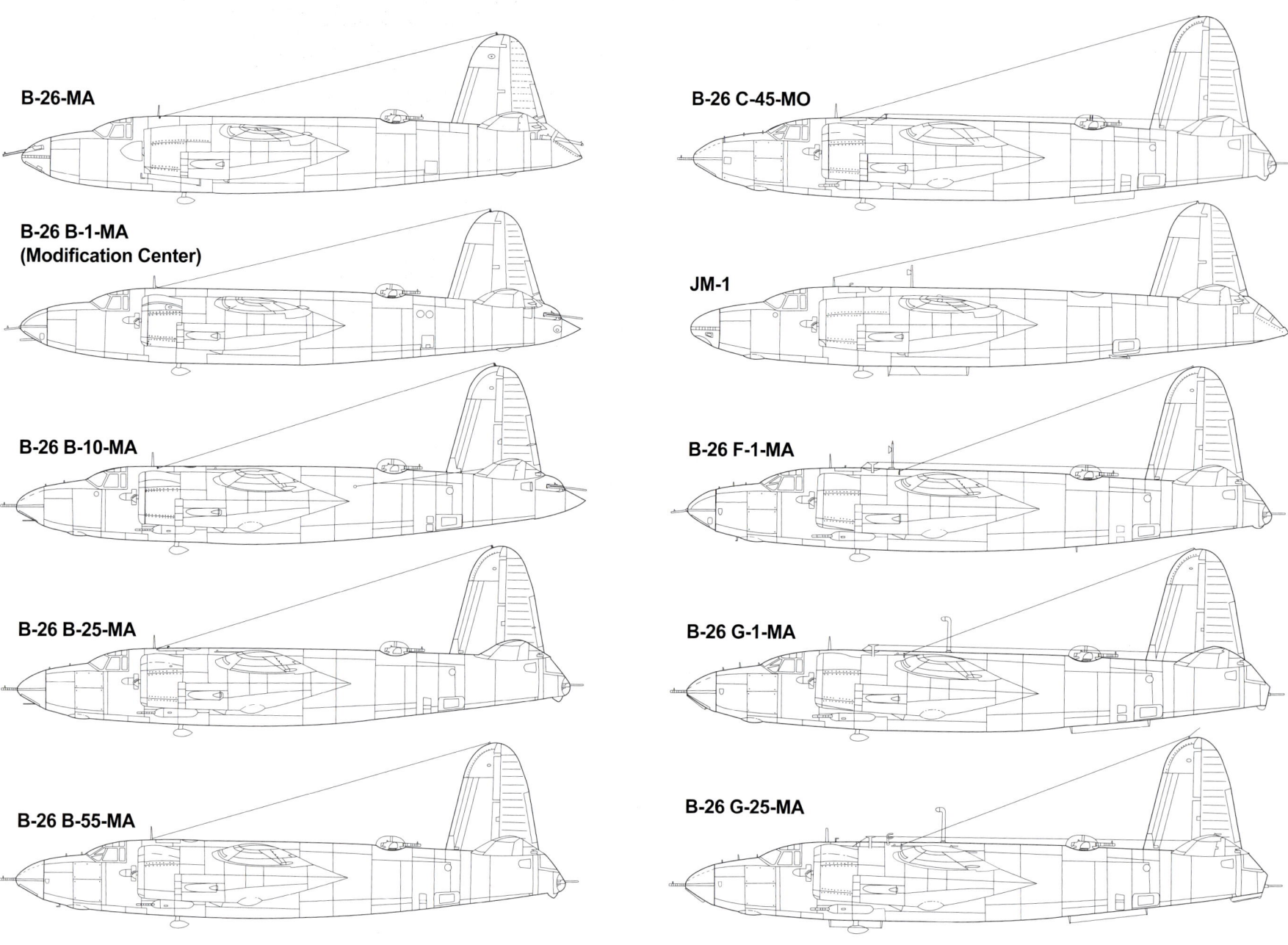

B-26 MA

In all, the U.S. Army Air Force received a total of 201 B-26 MAs (40-1361 through 40-1561). The first four Marauders were accepted on 22 February 1941 and were quickly allocated to the 22nd Bomb Group at Langley Field in Virginia. Only the first few B-26s were delivered in natural silver, while the main part of this batch received a camouflage with dark olive drab on the upper and neutral gray on the lower surfaces. These Marauders carried large national markings with a diameter of 56 inches on the rear fuselage.

Almost immediately after the delivery of the first B-26s to the Army Air Force, the Marauder began to pick up the reputation of being a killer, a reputation that would dog it throughout its career. The initial testing of the Marauder had been with fully armed and equipped aircraft, but the new B-26s arrived at Langley Field minus government-supplied equipment such as armament or radios. The change in the center-of-gravity made the Marauders nose heavy and a rash of nose gear failures followed. Martin strengthened the nose wheel strut, but it was not until full armament was added that the problem disappeared. Next, Marauders began crashing on take-off. The trouble was traced to failure of the electrically operated Curtis propeller. The airscrew would occasionally lose control and feather at the instant of highest demand – at take off. This problem was traced to faulty maintenance. The new Martin design also suffered from leaky hydraulic lines and clogged fuel lines. Since the Martin 250 CE turret was not available in the requested quantities, most B-26s were delivered to the Army Air Force without this turret.

Only a few modifications were introduced in the production line of the B-26-MA: the triangular windshield in the Plexiglas nose was replaced with an oval one. All B-26-MAs were delivered with a whip shaped VHF antenna mounted on the lower port nose section, but this feature was deleted on most Marauders during operations with the 22nd Bomb Group or the transition-training units. Hard landings wrinkled the skin on the rear fuselage of a number of B-26s. These aircraft were returned to the factory for reinforcement of the fuselage and new B-26s coming off the production line were equipped with these reinforcements as well. A few B-26s had the tear-drop shaped radio compass mounted on top of the fuselage, just behind the antenna mast, but on the majority of the aircraft, the radio compass covering was mounted on the lower centerline of the fuselage, just behind the nose wheel bay.

The first B-26-MAs left the assembly lines of the Glenn L. Martin Company at Middle River in Baltimore in silver overall, while the main part of the 201 Marauders manufactured in the first production block were camouflaged. The first four Marauders were accepted by the Army Air Corps on 22 February 1941. These first B-26-MAs ever built had the national markings applied on both sides of the wing upper surfaces. The B-26-MA nearest camera lacks the national marking on the rear fuselage, while all other Marauders have the initial large national marking with a diameter of 56 inches applied on the rear fuselage. Most of these early B-26-MAs were immediately transferred to the 22nd Bomb Group at Langley Field in Virginia. The boxcars in the background belong to the Baltimore & Ohio Railroad, which had its headquarter at Baltimore. (GLMMAM)

The majority all 201 B-26-MAs were camouflaged at Martin's Little River assembly line in Baltimore. The upper surfaces were painted in olive drab, the lower surfaces in neutral gray. This Marauder carried the initial large national marking with a diameter of 56 inches on the rear fuselage. On 15 May 1942 an order was issued to delete the Red dot from the American national marking in order to avoid confusion with Japanese planes. The lettering "Army" has here been applied under the left wing. (GLMMAM)

The second B-26-MA built (40-1362) was delivered from the Middle River plant at Baltimore in natural silver, but was subsequently repainted in olive drab on the upper and neutral gray on the lower surfaces. This was the first Marauder actually delivered to the Army Air Corps. This B-26-MA belly landed in a corn field near Patterson Field, Ohio, on 8 August 1941 after losing an engine. The small air intake on the lower engine cowling is evident. (GLMMAM)

This B-26-MA (40-1373) is armed with a 1,949-lb Bliss Leavitt Mark XIII Model 1 torpedo on a centerline-mounted rack. The weight of the torpedo was borne by cables that ran from shackles inside the bomb-bay. This Marauder belonged to 73rd Bomb Squadron that operated in November 1942 from a provisional air strip at Adak island on the Aleutians. At that time, the 73rd Bomb Squadron was part of the 42nd Bomb Group. The unit rarely saw action against Japanese vessels in the Aleutians. (Alain Pelletier)

Bettsy rolled out as the fourth Marauder from the Martin assembly line and had been accepted by the Army Air Corps on 22 February 1941. This B-26-MA (40-1364) briefly flew with the 22nd Bomb Group until a nose wheel failure on 3 April 1941 required a repair of the aircraft. The single window wiper attached on the upper cockpit frame is a field modification. The nickname *Bettsy* was painted on the Marauder after its service with the 22nd Bomb Group. (Jack K. Havener)

22nd Bomb Group

The Marauder launched its combat career Down Under – in Australia – in early 1942. A total of 51 disassembled Marauders sailed by ship from California to Hawaii, where they were reassembled and then flown over the rest of the Pacific to Australia. A total of 48 B-26s from the pioneering 22nd Bomb Group arrived at their final destination. The first mission was flown from Townsville in the Northern Queensland against Japanese-held Rabaul in New Britain on 5 April 1942. Nine B-26s took part in this 2,600-mile round trip. During April and May 1942, as part of the 5th Air Force, the 22nd Bomb Group flew a total of 16 missions against Rabaul.

On 15 May 1942 an order was issued to delete the Red dot from the U.S. national marking in order to avoid confusion with enemy planes. Otherwise, the 22nd Bomb Group continued to carry the large original national markings with a diameter of 56 inches. On most of the aircraft the serial number was applied in yellow on the rear fuselage behind the national marking. For a while, the 22nd Bomb Group continued to carry the red-white rudder and the blue bar on the horizontal stabilizer, but in the course of the war, the rudders were repainted in dark olive drab.

After its arrival in Australia, the 22nd Bomb Group made some distinctive field modifications on its Marauder fleet. Most B-26s had the rear glazing of the tail turret removed, allowing the gunner a better field of fire. Two small rectangular observation windows were added over the lower waist window. A number of 22nd Bomb Group Marauders had an additional Browning M-2 0.50 caliber machine gun mounted in either the port or starboard upper Plexiglas nose. There were even some Marauders that had two additional machine gun stations on both sides of the nose. Tail gunners often exchanged their 25-round magazines for those with 100 rounds, that had been borrowed from the B-17 Flying Fortress. In order to gain additional range, a 250-gallon fuel tank was installed in the rear bomb bay.

In January 1943 the 22nd Bomb Group was taken out of action, since only 32 B-26 remained operational and the Army Air Corps had decided to replace the B-26 by the North American B-25 Mitchell in the Pacific Theater of Operation. But this was not the end of Marauder operation in Australia. The 19th Bomb Squadron – being a part of the 22nd Bomb Group – volunteered to go back into action during July 1943 with the best of the surviving B-26s. Stripped of all camouflage and known as the "Silver Fleet," these veteran aircraft had the leading edges of their vertical and horizontal tailplanes painted black and also featured a black anti glare panel. The national marking on the fuselage was reduced in size and relocated further aft. The B-26s of the "Silver Fleet" flew their last mission on 9 January 1944. The remaining aircraft were all flown for storage to Eagle Farm depot near Brisbane, Australia, and eventually broken up.

Most B-26s serving with the 22nd Bomb Group in Australia had the serial number painted in Yellow on the rear fuselage. After the U.S. entered the war with Japan, the Marauders retained their large 56-inch national markings, but deleted the Red dot in the White star. Optimistically christened *Shamrock*, this B-26-MA (40-1437) unfortunately ran out of luck on 17 August 1942, when strafing Japanese fighters destroyed her at Port Moresby in New Guinea. (Steve Birdsall)

The 19th Squadron stripped the camouflage from all their ships and became the "Silver Fleet." The 19th Bomb Squadron as part of the 22nd Bomb Group flew their all silver B-26s between July 1943 and early January 1944. The B-26 nearest camera (40-1516) nicknamed *Calamity Jane* was scrapped at Eagle Farm depot near Brisbane (Australia) in early 1944. The white rectangle to each side of the national insignia star was introduced on all Army Air Force and Navy aircraft on 28 June 1943. (John Stanaway)

B-26-MA (40-1503) makes a Stateside practice flight, wearing pre-war national markings. This Marauder was shipped as deck cargo to Hawaii and was then flown across the Pacific to Australia. The 22nd Bomb Group lost this aircraft on 2 November 1942 when a tire blew during the landing at Loloki airstrip, New Guinea. (USAF)

22nd Bomb Group Development

B-26-MA

B-26-MA (22nd Bomb Group Modification)

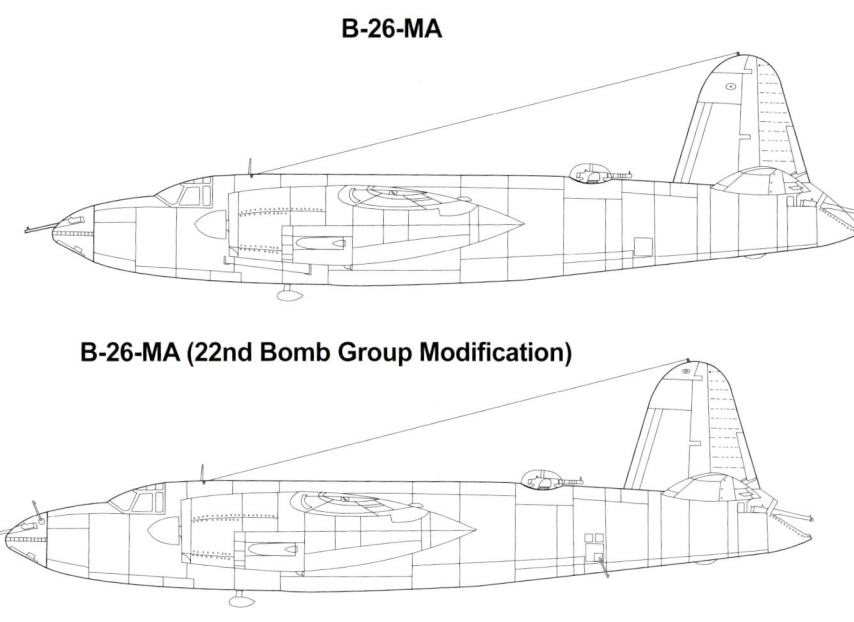

A part of the 19th Bomb Squadron's "Silver Fleet," B-26-MA (40-1432) *Little Audrey* has black propeller blades with Yellow tips. This B-26-MA also features the elliptical windshield in the Plexiglas nose that became standard on most B-26-MAs. *Little Audrey* was scrapped at Eagle Farm depot near Brisbane, Australia, in early 1944, after the "Silver Fleet" had phased out its Marauders. (Steve Birdsall)

Still featuring its original red-white rudder as well as the blue bar on the vertical stabilizer, B-26-MA (40-1510) *Wild Willie* of the 22nd Bomb Group, 33rd Bomb Squadron, rests at on an airstrip at Port Moresby, New Guinea. *Wild Willie* was damaged at Port Moresby by Japanese bombs and strafing on 4 July 1942. (Steve Birdsall)

A distinctive field modification carried out by the 22nd Bomb Group on its B-26-MAs was the removal of the rear glazing of the tail turret, allowing the gunner a better field of fire. Another modification was the introduction of two small rectangular observation windows added over the lower waist window. (Australian War Memorial)

Another member of the "Silver Fleet," B-26-MA *Fury* (40-1415), previously flew with the 33rd Bomb Squadron, 22nd Bomb Group, but began operating with the 19th Squadron in July 1943. *Fury* flew 25 missions with the "Silver Fleet" and was subsequently scrapped at Eagle Farm depot near Brisbane, Australia, during early 1944. (John Stanaway)

Major Walter Greer (left) and M/Sgt. Fuller pose with B-26-MA (40-1488) shortly after the newly devised "Silver Fleet" unit flash was applied to this Marauder. Major Greer had selected the nickname *Heckling Hare* for this particular B-26-MA. The aircraft was scrapped in Brisbane, Australia, in January 1944. (John Stanaway)

B-26 A-MA

The B-26 A-MA was a modified version of the B-26-MA, with which it appeared externally identical. The first examples of the B-26 A-MA were delivered in October 1941. Under the contract number AC-13243 only 29 B-26 A-MAs were built: (41-7345 through 41-7365, 41-7368, 41-7431 and 41-7477 through 41-7483). The B-26 A-MA had fittings for an auxiliary fuel tank in the aft bomb bay as well as improved armor protection for the crew. On the B-26 A-MA all of the 0.30-caliber machine guns were replaced by Browning M-2 0.50-caliber machine guns. The Browning M-2 was the defensive weapon most widely used on American medium and heavy bombers. In its rear bomb bay doors, the B-26 A-MA also had two square windows with an aperture in the center to serve as a machine gun position. Most R-2800-5 powerplants in these B-26 A-MAs were license built by the Ford Motor Company.

The B-26 was the only aircraft in the USAAF inventory ever to carry torpedoes. The B-26 A-MA received provision to carry a Bliss-Leavitt Mark XIII Model 1 torpedo, weighing 1,949 pounds, on a centerline-mounted rack. Two cables that passed through apertures in the closed bomb bay doors secured the torpedo. Air Corps crews were given a crash torpedo course by Navy instructors at North Island Navy Base at San Diego.

All B-26-MAs were delivered with large 56-inch national markings, but the smaller, 30-inch national markings on the B-26 A-MA were relocated further aft on the fuselage.

B-26 A-1-MA

The B-26 A-1-MA followed the B-26 A-MA on the production line at the Glenn L. Martin Company in Baltimore. The only difference from the previous variant was the introduction of the Pratt & Whitney R-2800-39 powerplant, replacing the R-2800-5 on the previous B-26 A-MA model. Both engines were of identical power rating. The R-2800-39s were in fact converted R-2800 S1A4G engines form a revoked Royal Air Force order. A total of 109 B-26 A-1-MAs (41-7366 and 41-7367, 41-7369 through 41-7430, 41-7432 through 41-7476) were built under the same contract AC-13243 as the B-26 A-MA. In all, 138 B-26 A-MAs and B-26 A-1-MAs were built, the last examples being delivered to the Army Air Corps in April 1942. None of these aircraft actually saw combat and most were assigned to Stateside training units. The gross weight of the B-26 A-1-MA rose to 28,376 pounds, and with a total fuel capacity of 1,462 gallons, the ferry range was increased to 2,600 miles.

Marauder I

The B-26 A-MA and B-26 A-1-MA were given under Lend-Lease aid to the Royal Air Force. A total of 71 aircraft were delivered (FK109 to FK160 and FK362 to FK380). This type received the designation Marauder I in Royal Air Force service. The Royal Air Force became the first foreign customer of the B-26. Like the B-26s of the USAAF, the British

The first batch of 52 Marauder I aircraft (FK109 to FK160) for the Royal Air Force were delivered in standard Army Air Corps camouflage, consisting of dark olive green on the upper surfaces and neutral gray on the lower surface. All Marauder I aircraft were supplied under the Lend-Lease Act, that had been signed on 11 March 1941 between the United States and Great Britain. (Martin Bowman)

Marauder I Development

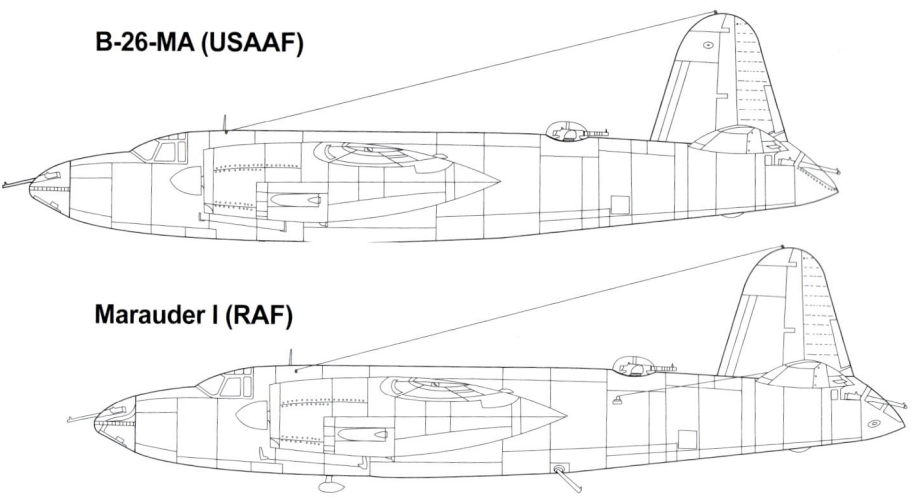

B-26-MA (USAAF)

Marauder I (RAF)

Marauder Is were built under contract AC-13243 by the Glenn L. Martin Company in Baltimore. The first Marauder I (FK138) arrived in Great Britain on 2 September 1942, being flown by Captain Don McVicar from Gander in Newfoundland to Prestwick in Scotland. A total of five Marauders crashed prior to delivery and seven were lost in transit.

The British Marauder I differed in a number of details, mainly in radio equipment, from the B-26 A-MA and B-26 A-1-MA. Also, the position light on the Marauder I was relocated from the tail fin to a position in the tail cone. These models also featured an antenna cable on each side, leading from an attachment point on the rear fuselage under the top turret to the leading edge of the horizontal stabilizer. The Royal Air Force Marauder Is continued to carry the whip shaped VHF antenna located on the lower port nose section after being assigned to combat units. All Army Air Corps units had removed this particular antenna. The first batch of 52 Marauder I (FK109 to FK160) were delivered in standard Army Air Corps camouflage, consisting dark olive green on the upper surfaces and neutral gray on the lower surface. The second batch of 19 Marauder Is (FK362 to FK380) saw combat in the Middle East with a sand and earth brown camouflage on the upper surfaces and light blue on the lower surfaces.

The Marauder I saw service with the No. 14 Squadron in the Middle East, where operations started in autumn 1942 out of Fâyid air base in Egypt. The unit was also active over the Bay of Tunis, and, in addition to bombing missions, the Squadron also dropped mines and torpedoes in the Aegean Sea. In early 1943, the Marauders of this unit were transferred to the North West African Coastal Air Force, where they performed shipping and weather reconnaissance sorties. In late 1943, detachments of the No. 14 Squadron started to operate from Italy, Sardinia, and Sicily, locating and shadowing enemy coastal vessels until an air-strike force arrived. The unit continued to play its role over the Mediterranean until autumn 1944, when the Squadron was ordered back to England.

Marauder I (FK375) *Dominion Revenge* carries the individual aircraft letter "D" in red on the rear fuselage as she flies missions from Fâyid air base in Egypt with the No. 14 Squadron in late 1942. The No. 14 Squadron was the only Royal Air Force unit that went into combat with the Marauder I. FK375 failed to return from its fourth mission, a torpedo armed reconnaissance flight over the Aegean Sea on 3 January 1943. (Martin Bowman)

One of the last examples of this block to be built, B-26 A-1-MA (41-7462) is seen here carrying a dummy torpedo. The Marauder could be also equipped with a real Bliss-Leavitt Mark XIII Model 1 torpedo on a centerline mounted pylon. In contrast to the early B-26-MA with 0.30-caliber machine guns, all B-26 A-MAs and B-26 A-1-MAs were equipped with Browning M-2 0.50-caliber weapons improving considerably the defense capacity of the Marauder. (Steve Birdsall)

FK138 became the first Marauder I to arrive in the United Kingdom when Captain Don McVicar flew the aircraft from Gander in Newfoundland to Prestwick in Scotland on 2 September 1942. USAAF crews had flown the Royal Air Force Marauders to Montréal, Canada, where they were handled over to British crews of the Ferry Command. FK138 went as "Red X" in June 1944 to No. 14 Squadron and crashed at Grottaglie, Italy, on takeoff for its 42nd mission on 21 September 1944. (Martin Bowman)

B-26 B-MA (factory)

The Martin B-26 B-MA boasted a number of modifications that eliminated various shortcomings of the previous B-26-MA and B-26 A-MA models. The single machine gun was replaced by a hand-operated turret with two Browning M-2 0.50-caliber weapons. The introduction of the stepped down tail position lengthened the fuselage by three inches to 58 feet 3 inches. The ammunition supply rose from the 400 rounds of the single Browning M-2 in the B-26 A-MA, to 1,600 rounds on the B-26 B-MA.

The spinners were deleted from the Curtis four-blade propellers on the B-26 B-MA. A vaulted window on starboard provided the navigator with an improved field of vision. The earlier B-26-MA and B-26 A-MA were all equipped with a square flush window. The lack of a spinner and the vaulted window were features that remained through the entire production cycle of the Marauder.

The B-26-MA and the B-26 A-MA had a 12-volt electrical system, which was changed to 24 volt on the B-26 B-MA. The B-26 B-MA received the Pratt & Whitney R-2800-41 Double Wasp engine with a take-off power of 1,920 h.p. – 70 h.p. more than the R-2800-39 in the B-26 A-1-MA. The R-2800-41 powerplant was a converted R-2800 2SB-G from a former Royal Air Force order. The R-2800-41 equipped B-26 B-MA received a larger air intake on the lower engine cowling than the previous B-26 A-MA models with the R-2800-39. A total of 307 B-26 B-MAs were built (41-17544 through 41-17624 and 41-17626 through 41-17851) between May 1942 and August 1942. These aircraft were built under contract AC-16137.

B-26 B-MA Development

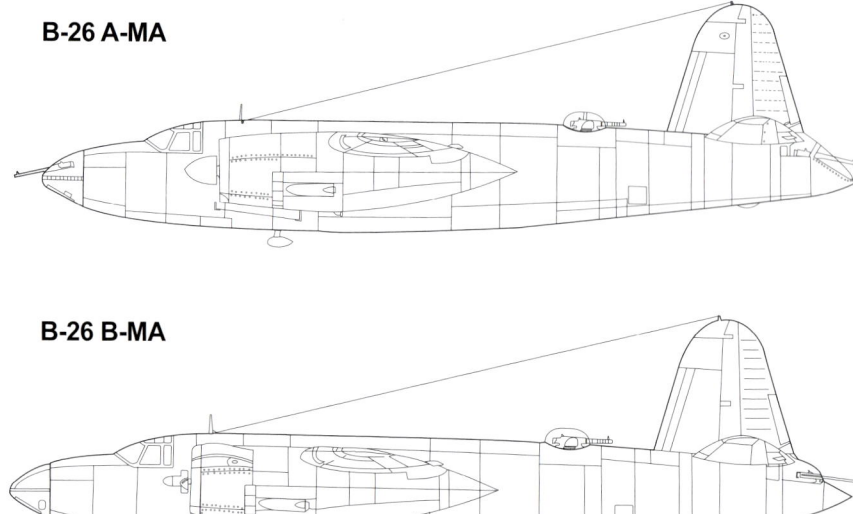

B-26 A-MA

B-26 B-MA

Freshly completed B-26 B-MAs wait for their propellers at the Glenn L. Martin factory field at Middle River in Baltimore in 13 May 1942. There was a shortage of Curtis propellers that forced the manufacturer to store the aircraft on the apron of the freshly built Plant 2. (Lockheed Martin)

B-26 B-1-MA (modified)

The B-26 B-1-MA was the first Marauder variant to see combat against Axis forces in North Africa. The B-26 B-1-MA was an unofficial designation of B-26 B-MAs converted by the Martin Modification Center at Offutt air base near Omaha, Nebraska. The 17th, 319th, and 320th Bomb Groups settled on their North African bases in late 1942. Before departing overseas, all the aircraft of these three pioneering Bomb Groups were heavily modified according to Army Air Corps specifications. The original Plexiglas nose was replaced by a transparent nose with a V-shaped brace behind the upper half molding. The flexible gun position was relocated to the center of this brace. The flexible nose gun with the Bell E-11 adapter was supported by a ball and socket and balanced by a bungee support at the aft end. On the out-of-factory B-26 B-MAs, this gun was located upward of the horizontal brace. An additional fixed Browning M-2 machine gun was mounted in the nose compartment. An ammunition box holding 135 rounds was fitted on the starboard interior of the new B-26 B-1-MA Plexiglas. The access hatch was moved from its original, starboard position to the port side. A canvas bag attached to the gun collected cases and links. With the introduction of the fixed machine gun, a tube for collecting and discharging spent cases was mounted on the lower port skin of the front fuselage. This tube was short lived and only introduced on the B-26 B-1-MAs that went overseas for combat. All further production blocks of the B-26 B had a canvas bag attached to the gun to collect cases and links of the fixed machine gun.

Out-of-the-factory B-26 B-MAs took over the small, centerline-mounted radio mast located on top of the fuselage from the B-26 A. On combat-modified B-26 B-1-MAs this rectangular antenna mast was replaced by a slightly taller, triangular antenna mast.

The Modification Center at Omaha followed the practice of the 22nd Bomb Group of deleting the whip VHF antenna that was located on factory-fresh Marauders on the port lower front fuselage section. In place of it, a retractable wire antenna was mounted on the port side, in front of the bomb bay. This wire antenna was attached to an external weight with a bulged shape. Unlike the wire antenna, the weight could not be fully retracted into the fuselage.

Factory-fresh B-26 B-MAs lacked the two circular windows located on both sides of the rear fuselage. The Modification Center cut out these two windows to enable the gunners to observe enemy fighters.

The position light was relocated to a place on the tail cone on combat-modified B-26 B-1-MAs. This arrangement was similar to that found on previously built Marauder Is of the Royal Air Force. On out-of-the-factory B-26 B-MAs, the position light was located on the upper portion of the vertical stabilizer.

The combat modified B-26 B-1-MA received enlarged carburetor air intakes designed to accept tropical sand filters. Two of these enlarged carburetor air intakes were located on top of each engine cowling and there was a small outlet located on the outer cowling. In order to travel overseas, provision was made for two 250-gallon ferry tanks that could be mounted for long-range flights in the rear bomb bay.

Lady Halitosis was an original B-26 B-1-MA (41-17765) of the 320th Bomb Group, 12th Air Force that carried out 43 missions over Tunisia, Sicily, and Sardinia. Assigned to the 441st Bomb Squadron, Lady Halitosis operated from Massicault (now Burj al-'Âmirî) in Tunisia. Afterwards, on 15 July 1943, she returned home to the United States, where on 26 August that year she paid a visit to Martin's Middle River Plant in Baltimore. (GLMMAM)

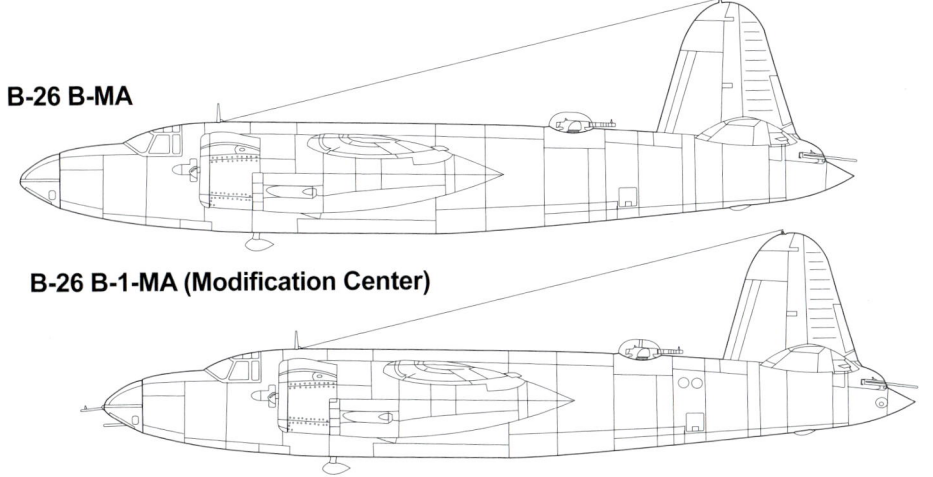

B-26 B-1-MA (Modified) Development

B-26 B-MA

B-26 B-1-MA (Modification Center)

Accurate German Flak over La Smala (Zamâlat as-Sawâsî) airfield on the east coast of Tunisia damaged this B-26 B-1-MA (41-17747), nicknamed *Earthquake McGoon* on 24 March 1943. This aircraft belonged to the 17th Bomb Group, 37th Bomb Squadron. The astrodome was rarely used by Marauder crews. The 17th Bomb Group arrived on 21 December 1942 at its home base Telergma (at-Talâghimah), Algeria, and flew its first combat mission exactly a week later. This Marauder had been modified according Army Air Corps guidelines in the Modification Center at Offutt air base near Omaha, Nebraska. None of the three Marauder Bomb Groups deployed to the North African theater of operations displayed any Squadron or Group marking in the early phase of operation. (Gino Künzle)

Nose Development

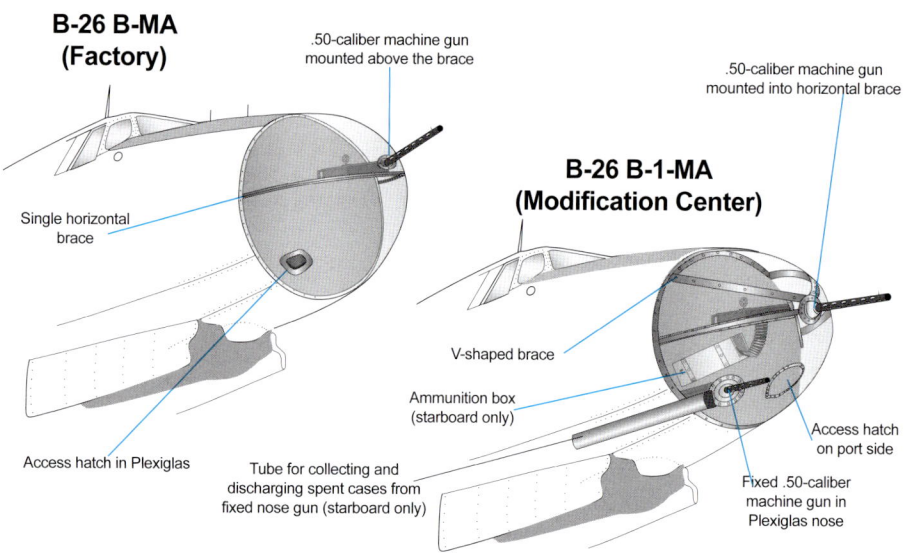

B-26 B-MA (Factory)
- Single horizontal brace
- .50-caliber machine gun mounted above the brace
- Access hatch in Plexiglas

B-26 B-1-MA (Modification Center)
- .50-caliber machine gun mounted into horizontal brace
- V-shaped brace
- Ammunition box (starboard only)
- Tube for collecting and discharging spent cases from fixed nose gun (starboard only)
- Access hatch on port side
- Fixed .50-caliber machine gun in Plexiglas nose

The last B-26 B-1-MA built, 41-17851 flew with the 320th Bomb Group after arrival in North Africa. The Yellow battle number had been over painted when the Marauder was turned over as a trainer to the Groupe de Bombardement I/22 "Maroc" of the Free French Air Forces at Telergma (at-Talâghimah), Algeria, in September 1943. The serial number had been relocated to the top and the Yellow identification band, a 320th Bomb Group identification marking, around the tail over painted. (Gino Künzle)

B-26 B-1-MA (Modified)

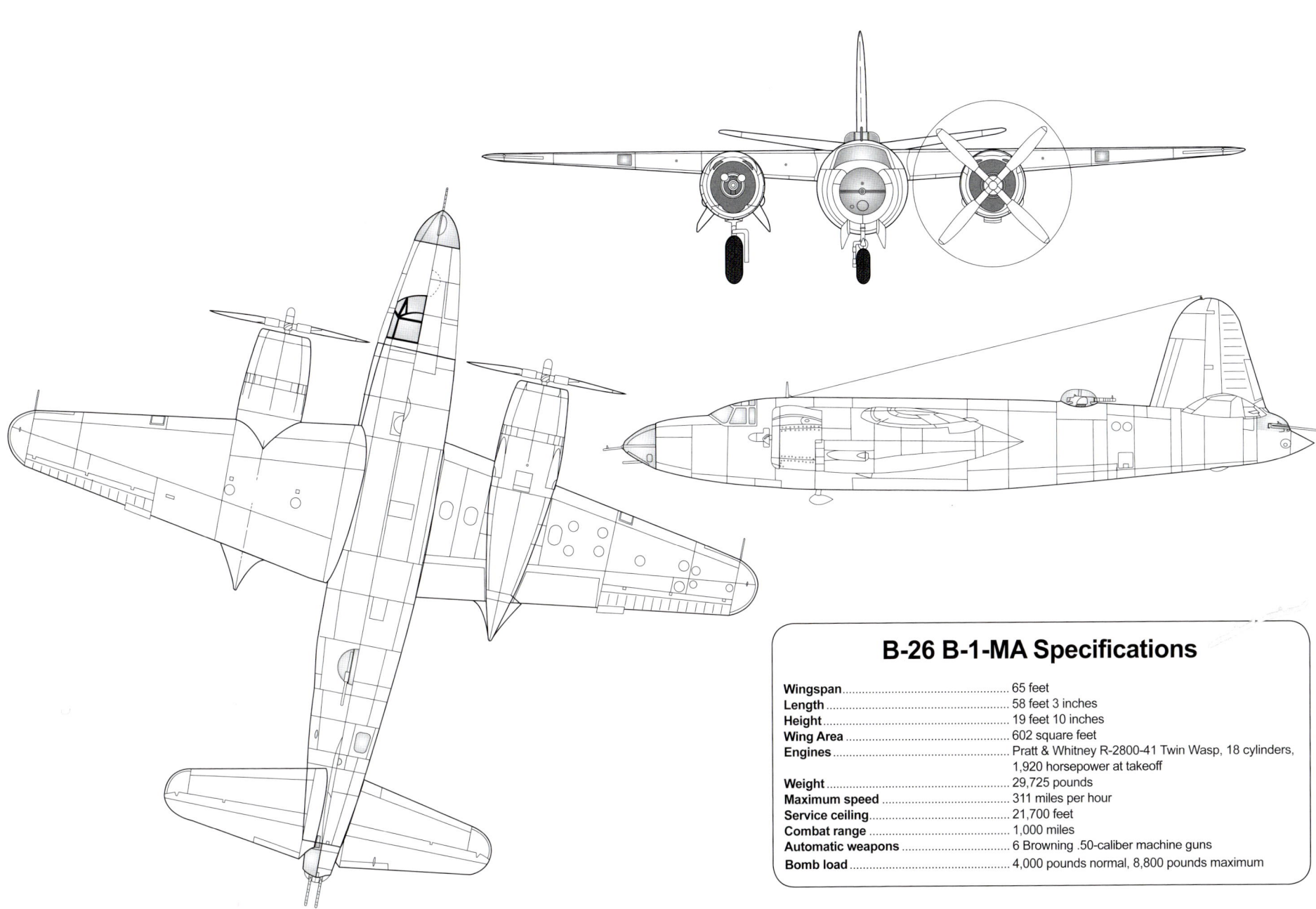

B-26 B-1-MA Specifications

Wingspan	65 feet
Length	58 feet 3 inches
Height	19 feet 10 inches
Wing Area	602 square feet
Engines	Pratt & Whitney R-2800-41 Twin Wasp, 18 cylinders, 1,920 horsepower at takeoff
Weight	29,725 pounds
Maximum speed	311 miles per hour
Service ceiling	21,700 feet
Combat range	1,000 miles
Automatic weapons	6 Browning .50-caliber machine guns
Bomb load	4,000 pounds normal, 8,800 pounds maximum

Luftwaffe B-26 B-1-MA

The German Luftwaffe received a nearly intact and brand new example of the Marauder long before the 12th Air Force started operating from North Africa against German and Italian held positions. Lt. Clarence C. Wall, piloting a B-26 B-1-MA (41-17790), was among other Marauder men of the 319th Bomb Group on a ferry flight from Iceland to Prestwick in Scotland. During this flight, the crew picked up a German homing signal by mistake and followed it through solid overcast towards German-occupied continental Europe. With all tanks nearly dry and one engine out of order due to fuel starvation, Lt. Clarence C. Wall decided to belly land on the beach – not knowing that he was putting down on the island of Noord Beveland in the Netherlands, some 40 miles away from Rotterdam – territory occupied by the German Wehrmacht since the Reich's Blitzkrieg victory in spring 1940.

This fatal error delivered a brand new Martin Marauder to the Luftwaffe on 3 October 1942 – albeit without its defensive armament. All machine guns and specialized service equipment had been removed from the aircraft at Goose Bay (Labrador) before the 319th Bomb Group started its journey across the Atlantic Ocean.

A salvage team under the command of Flughafenbereichsingenieur (chief airfield engineer) Erich Reiche arrived from the large Luftwaffe air base at Gilze-Rijen. The helpless B-26 B-1-MA got back on its wheels with the help of large, inflatable hoisting cushions that were placed under the wings. The bent Curtis four-blade propeller was replaced on the spot with a three-blade propeller with a spinner. The origins of the propellers are still unknown, but it is assumed that the airscrews must have been of American origin as well.

The U.S. national markings were replaced by those of the German Luftwaffe and a yellow identification band was painted on the rear fuselage. The lower wing tips and part of the vertical stabilizer also received yellow paint, but in the main the original Army Air Corps camouflage remained untouched.

On its own power generated by the two Pratt & Whitney R-2800-41 Double Wasp engines, the Marauder taxied through sand hills to a flat, but unprepared field on the island of Noord Beveland that allowed a safe take off to Gilze-Rijen airfield. After arrival at the Dutch base, the Yellow fuselage band was broadened. The aircraft remained at Gilze-Rijen until early 1943, when a pair of intact Curtis propellers from another captured Marauder became available for the Luftwaffe B-26.

The large Erprobungsstelle der Luftwaffe (Luftwaffe Test and Experimental Center) began evaluation of the B-26 at Rechlin and Lärz air bases during June 1943. In July, while the B-26 was allocated to the E2 Department of the Erprobungsstelle, which was responsible for the flight evaluation, the aircraft received a generator. On 2 November 1943, the sole Luftwaffe B-26 in airworthy condition went on display as part of an exhibition of latest Luftwaffe innovations and captured aircraft at Rechlin. At about this time the sole Marauder in Luftwaffe service disappears from the records; the final fate of Lt. Clarence C. Wall's unfortunate ship remains unknown.

Lt. Clarence C. Wall bellied this B-26 B-1-MA (41-17790) 3 October 1942 on the beach of Noord Beveland island in German occupied Holland due to dry fuel tanks and delivered the Luftwaffe a nearly intact Marauder. The port Curtis propeller had to feather because of the fuel starvation. For the ferry flight from Iceland to Prestwick in Scotland, all armament had been removed from the B-26 belonging to the 319th Bomb Group in order to save weight. (Erich Reiche via Karl Kössler)

The former 319th Bomb Group Marauder rests at Gilze-Rijen, a major Luftwaffe air base in the Netherlands. The German Luftwaffe received this brand new B-26 B-1-MA (41-17790) some two months before the 12th Air Force started combat operation in the North African theater of operation against Axis power. The Marauder retains in its original Army Air Corps camouflage, the American national markings having been over painted in slightly lighter green. (Erich Reiche via Karl Kössler)

Members of the German salvage team from Gilze-Rijen run up the two Pratt & Whitney R-2800-41 Double Wasp to get the Marauder, already given Luftwaffe markings, away from the beach at Noord Beveland in the Netherlands, where the B-26 B-1-MA had belly landed on 3 October 1942. The soldiers are building a path trough the sand with the help of wooden planks. (Erich Reiche via Karl Kössler)

The B-26 B-1-MA (41-17790) successfully accomplished its ferry flight to Gilze-Rijen air base. The original Curtis four-blade propellers had bent in the belly landing and were exchanged for three-blade propellers. (Erich Reiche via Karl Kössler)

German ground crew escape from the strong prop wash generated by nearly 4,000 h.p. of the two Pratt & Whitney R-2800-41 Double Wasp engines. The B-26 B-1-MA has already been painted in Luftwaffe markings and wears a narrow Yellow identification band that was broadened after the aircraft's arrival at the Gilze-Rijen airbase. No armament was carried when the ship fell into enemy hands. (Erich Reiche via Karl Kössler)

Luftwaffe Propeller Development

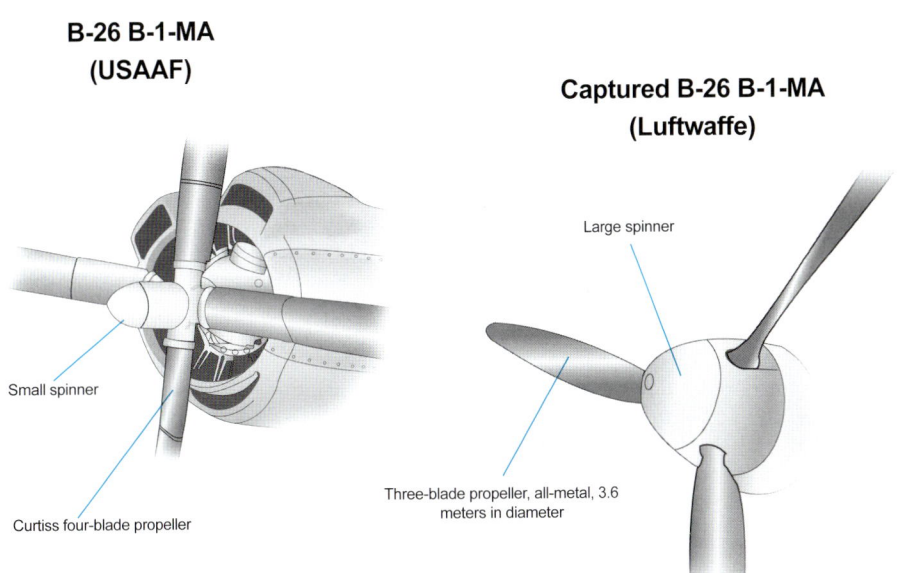

B-26 B-1-MA (USAAF) — Small spinner, Curtiss four-blade propeller

Captured B-26 B-1-MA (Luftwaffe) — Large spinner, Three-blade propeller, all-metal, 3.6 meters in diameter

B-26 B-2 to B-4-MA

The B-26 B-2-MA was externally identical to the B-26 B-MA. There were a total of 95 examples built under contract AC 16137 (41-17852 through 41-17946). These aircraft were modified to a combat-fit stage in the same manner as the B-26 B-1-MA, with the exception of the tube for collecting and discharging spent cases from the fixed Browning M-2 0.50-caliber machine guns. This tube was not fitted on the B-26 B-2-MA; instead a box to collect the spent cases was mounted in the interior of the nose section. The box would be emptied once the aircraft had returned to base. The B-26 B-2-MA became the first variant of the Marauder to reach the 8th Air Force in England for missions against occupied Europe. A total of nine B-26 B-2-MAs arrived in March 1943 with the 322nd Bomb Group. The original D-8 bomb sight mounted at the production line proved unsuitable and was replaced on all 8th Air Force Marauders by the Norden M-7 bomb sight during summer 1943.

The B-26 B-3-MA was the first variant on which the production line at the Middle River plant in Baltimore had introduced the large carburetor intakes as well as the small outlet on the outer engine cowling. These large carburetor intakes housed tropical sand filters and had been mounted on the previous B-26 B-1-MA and B-2-MA as a modification only. The B-26 B-3-MA variant received the Pratt & Whitney R-2800-43 Double Wasp powerplant with identical performance to that of the R-2800-41 of the B-26 B-1-MA and B-2-MA. There were only 28 examples of the B-26 B-3-MA built (41-17625 and 41-17947 through 41-17973).

The B-26 B-4-MA was the first Marauder variant to be equipped with a lengthened nose wheel strut that made necessary a bulge in the front portion of the nose wheel door as well as in a portion of the front of the nose wheel bay. This modification increased wing incidence and lift at takeoff and shortened the takeoff run. Also on the production line, one circular observation window was fitted on each side of the rear fuselage. Previous Marauder variants lacked this window and were subsequently modified with two circular windows. Deleted from the B-26 B-4-MA were the two square windows on the rear bomb bay door. These windows had served on previous variants as a gun position. For low-level operation with the 322nd Bomb Group, 8th Air Force, a number of B-26 B-4-MAs received an N-6 reflector gun sight fixed to the decking behind the starboard windshield for use by the co-pilot. Retractable circular air ventilators were introduced under both sides of the cockpit compartment. A total of 211 B-26 B-4-MA aircraft (41-17974 through 41-18184) were built. Production lasted from October 1942 until the end of that year.

Hell Cat became the very first Marauder to pass the 50th mission mark. This B-26 B-2-MA (41-117903) flew with the 17th Bomb Group. The mission symbols were painted on a black board under the cockpit. No Squadron or Group marking was applied until July 1943 to Marauders serving with the 42nd Bomb Wing, 12th Air Force in North Africa. At the time of its 50th mission, *Hell Cat* was based at Sedrata (Sidrâtah) in northeastern Algeria. *Hell Cat* passed this magic mark in early June 1943 and was subsequently flown back to the United States. (USAF)

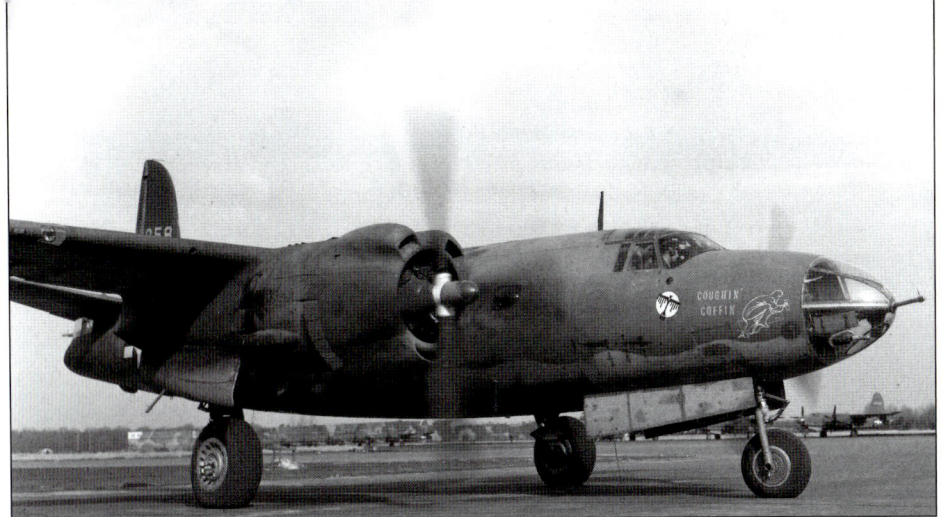

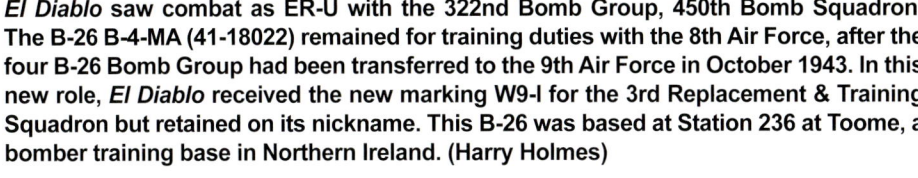

B-26 B-2-MA (41-17858) *Coughin' Coffin* flies with the 17th Bomb Group, 34th Bomb Squadron. The B-26 B-2-MA became the first block from which the fairing for the tube for collecting and discharging spent cases on the starboard nose was deleted. *Coughin' Coffin* accomplished its 50th mission on 11 July 1943 with Lt. Fred Mehner at the controls and subsequently returned to the United States, where it visited the Middle River plant in Baltimore on 9 December 1943. (GLMMAM)

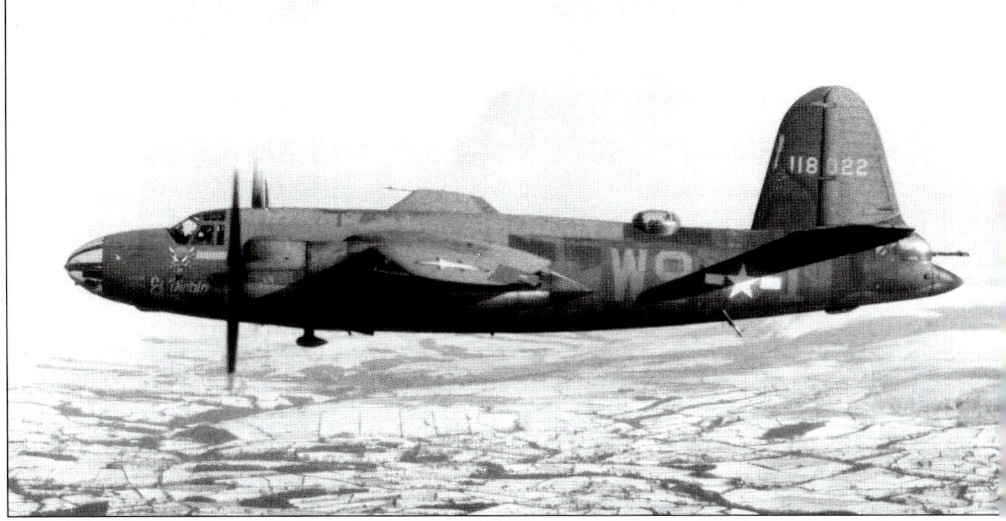

El Diablo saw combat as ER-U with the 322nd Bomb Group, 450th Bomb Squadron. The B-26 B-4-MA (41-18022) remained for training duties with the 8th Air Force, after the four B-26 Bomb Group had been transferred to the 9th Air Force in October 1943. In this new role, *El Diablo* received the new marking W9-I for the 3rd Replacement & Training Squadron but retained on its nickname. This B-26 was based at Station 236 at Toome, a bomber training base in Northern Ireland. (Harry Holmes)

Nose Wheel Development

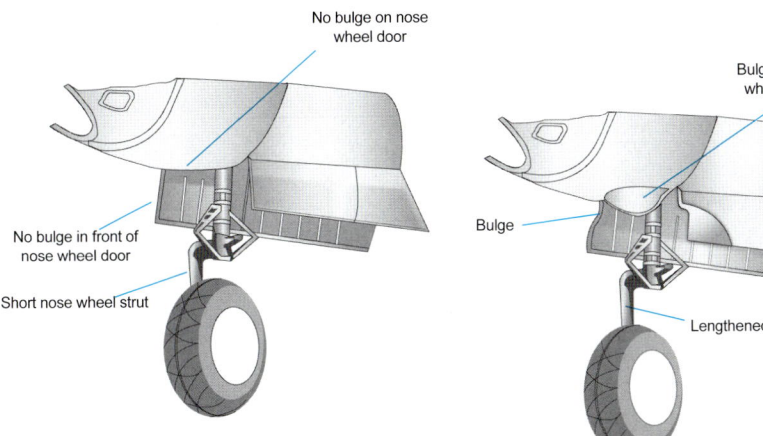

B-26 B-3-MA
B-26 B-4-MA
No bulge on nose wheel door
No bulge in front of nose wheel door
Short nose wheel strut
Bulge on nose wheel doors
Bulge
Lengthened nose wheel strut

Some war-weary Marauders, like *The Fryjack Airlines Inc.,* a B-26 B-2-MA (41-17875) of the 17th Bomb Group, 12th Air Force, were converted for transport duty in North Africa. All armament was removed from the nose. (Jack Gordon via Jack K. Havener)

Flagship
The
FRYJACK AIRLINES
INC.

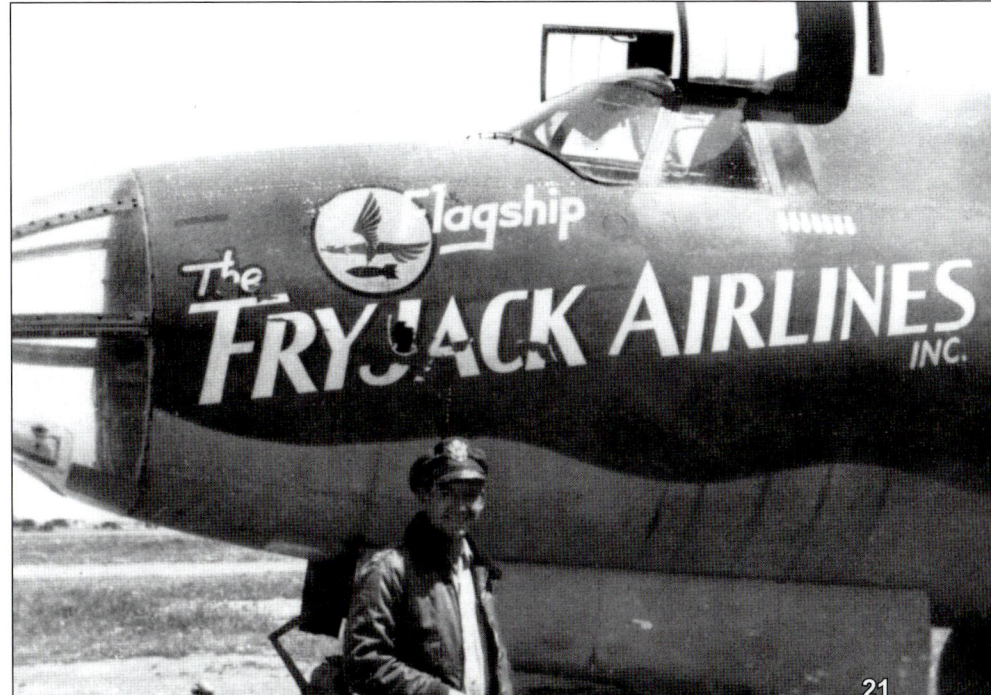

B-26 B-10-MA

The short-wing Marauder resulted in a high wing loading, which was responsible for high take off speed as well as a long take off and landing run. Coupled with poor directional stability and slow control response, the Marauder was in many aspects a "hot" aircraft with fighter behavior and needed well trained pilots. Experienced pilots who had already flown two-engine bombers such as the B-18 Bolo or the B-25 Mitchell could master the B-26 with little difficulty, but for green pilots with just a couple of hours on the single-engine AT-6 Texan in the Advanced Flying Training, the Marauder was literally a killer. The accident rate during training was so excessive, that the Truman Committee recommended that B-26 production be stopped. To solve all these serious shortcomings, the Glenn L. Martin Company undertook a major redesign of the Marauder, that resulted in the B-26 B-10-MA. Production started in January 1943 and a total of 150 examples (41-18185 through 41-18334) were delivered.

The wing loading was reduced by a new wing with an increased wingspan of 71 feet – six feet longer than the B-26 B-4-MA wingspan. The wing area rose from 602 square feet to 658 square feet. A slight dihedral angle was incorporated and the split flaps were replaced by slotted ones. On the lower surfaces of the slotted flaps, a fairing for the hinge was introduced. The tab mounted on the trailing edge of the outer flaps was now incorporated into the flap. The Pitot tube was offset from the wing tip. All short-wing Marauders carried one position light each on the upper and lower surfaces of the wing tip, the B-26 B-10-MA had a single position light incorporated in the outer wing leading edge of the wing tip. Three landing lights were introduced on the lower port wing surface of the B-26 B-10-MA. These lights could be lowered when required, but were usually retracted in the wing. The short-wing Marauder had none of these lights. The layout for the circular access panels on the wing undersurfaces was altered on the B-26 B-10-MA. The increased wing area reduced take off and landing speed, and on the other hand, it cut the top speed of the B-26 B-10-MA by about 35 miles per hour down to 282 mph.

All short-wing Marauders were equipped with a solid access panel on the upper rear engine cowling. The long-wing B-26 B-10-MA had a panel with eight slots in it.

The B-26 B-10-MA was the first variant to be equipped with bulged main wheel doors. The previous short-wing Marauders were all equipped with flush mail wheel doors. The bulges became necessary after the introduction of 50-inch tires, replacing the 47-inch tires on the main wheels of the B-26 B-4-MA.

In order to improve the poor directional stability of the B-26, the tail was enlarged by 20 inches and the rudder area was increased as well. The fairing for the port hinge between the rudder and trim tab were offset to a position above of that on the B-26 B-4-MA. The B-26 B-10-MA lacked the tail bumper that featured on all short-wing B-26s. On all short-wing B-models of the Marauder the position light was relocated from the tail to a position on the tail cone as a Modification Center procedure. On the B-26 B-10-MA, the position light remained on the tail tip.

Following the combat experience over Europe and North Africa, the small waist gun position on the lower rear fuselage was enlarged on the B-26 B-10-MA to provide the gunners with a greater field of fire. In addition, two wind deflectors were mounted on each waist gun position. Each waist gun had an ammunition supply of 240 rounds. The guns were fed through a flexible track from an ammunition box above the guns.

All short-wing B-models of the Marauder left the production line at Middle River with a Plexiglas nose without braces and also lacked a fixed Browning M-2 in the starboard nose. These features were all introduced at the Modification Center before these B-26s went overseas for combat. The B-26 B-10-MA became the first variant on which the production line in Baltimore incorporated the fixed machine gun and the V-shaped brace behind the upper half molding. The production line fitted a whip shaped VHF antenna on all short-wing B-26s, but the whip antenna was deleted at Modification Centers. The B-26 B-10-MA became the first variant on which the production line deleted this antenna, fitting instead the extended antenna wire plus the external aerial weight on the port lower fuselage.

The B-26 B-10-MA also enjoyed a major improvement in firepower. Four package Browning M-2 0.50-caliber machine guns were fitted on the outer fuselage, two to a side. Two pin-shaped aiming devices were applied on the upper nose section. A fairing protected each of these removable machine guns, which were fed ammunition from inside the fuselage by means of flexible tracks. There was an ammunition supply of 250 rounds for the two upper guns and 200 rounds for the lower guns. Cases and links were ejected directly into the airstream. While most 8th and 9th Air Force B-26s did not touch the package guns, many Bomb Groups serving with the 12th Air Force removed either two or all four machine guns as a field modification.

The first B-26 B-10-MAs arrived in Britain during April 1943 as original equipment of the 322nd Bomb Group and the 323rd Bomb Group.

B-26 B-10-MA Development

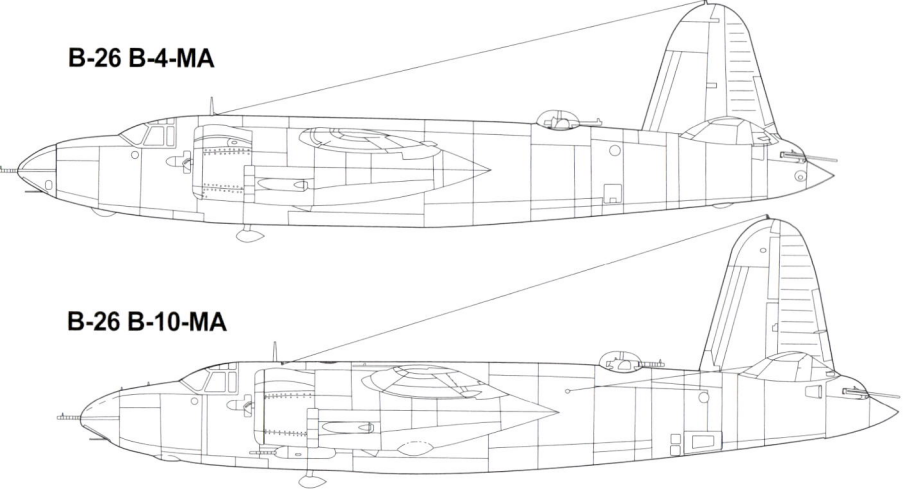

B-26 B-4-MA

B-26 B-10-MA

22

This B-26 B-10-MA (41-18288) displays no Group or Squadron marking, in keeping with the standard practice followed by the 42nd Bomb Wing, 12th Air Force until July 1943, when a 10-inch-wide band was painted on the rear fuselage, close to the tail gunner's position. It was not until October 1943, that the Marauder units of the 12th Air Force in the Mediterranean Theater introduced the large, two-digit battle number on the tail fin. This aircraft belonged to the 320th Bomb Group, 444th Bomb Squadron and subsequently received the individual battle number "62." This particular Marauder crashed on 2 September 1944. (Howard R. Baxter via Jack K. Havener)

Battle Number 93 is a B-26 B-10-MA (41-18292) that belonged to the 320th Bomb Group, 12th Air Force. Christened *Idiots Delight*, this Marauder carries the national markings that were introduced during August 1943. (Dave Mickelson via Jack K. Havener)

Gremlins' Castle was a B-26 B-10-MA (41-18264) that once flew as Battle Number 39 with the 17th Bomb Group, 37th Bomb Squadron. This Marauder accomplished a total of 72 missions in the Mediterranean Theater of Operations before the it was sent home for a War Bond selling tour in the United States. (GLMMAM)

Wing Development

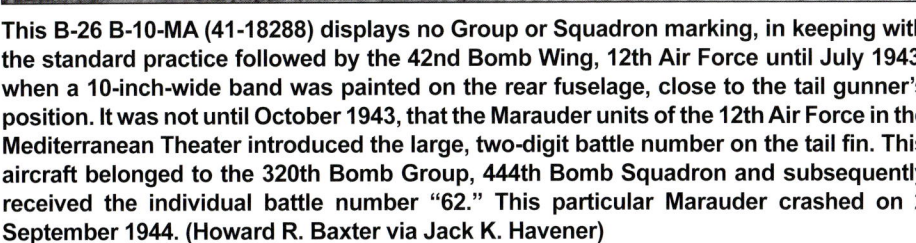

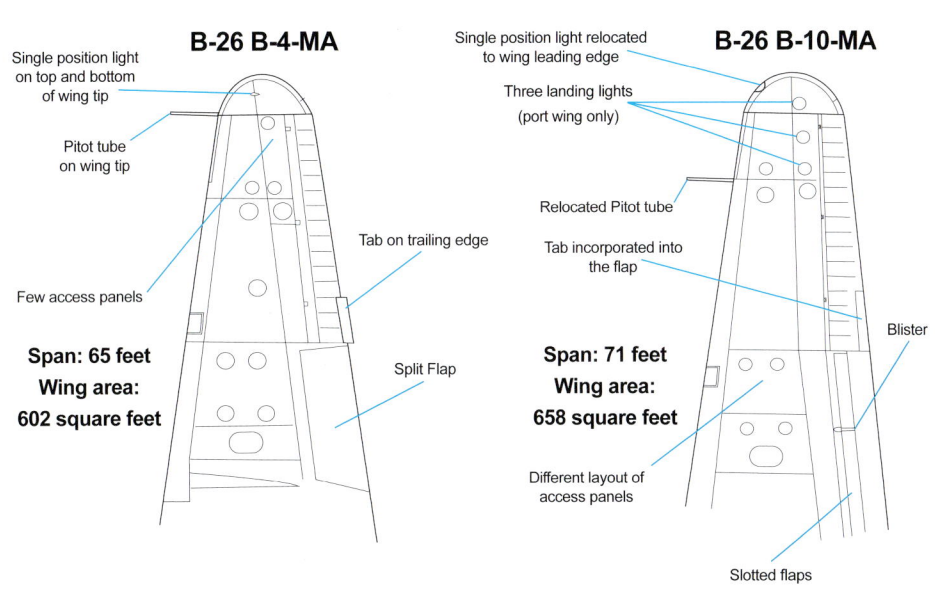

Gun Package Development

B-26 B-4-MA

B-26 B-10-MA

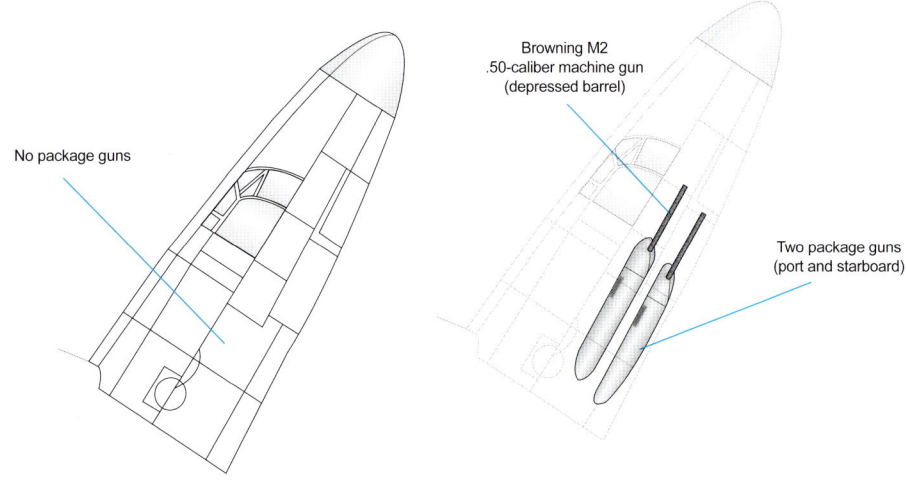

No package guns

Browning M2 .50-caliber machine gun (depressed barrel)

Two package guns (port and starboard)

Colonel Rebel was a B-26 B-10-MA (41-18289) that flew with the unit code PN-W for the 322nd Bomb Group, 449th Bomb Squadron. This unit was based at Station 485 Andrews Field in England. The white triangle on each side of the star insignia was added in late June 1943. (Gino Künzle)

Rain Check once flew for the 319th Bomb Group, 437th Bomb Squadron with the Battle Number 08. This B-26 B-10-MA (41-18202) had been transferred to the Groupe de Bombardement I/22 "Maroc" of the Free French Air Force based at Telergma (at-Talâghimah), Algeria, in September 1943. An alloy sheet had been wrapped on the lower half of the nose as a temporary repair measure. Both gun packages had been removed from this Marauder. (Gino Künzle)

This battered 320th Bomb Group B-26 B-10-MA awaits in autumn 1944 clearance for take off from Decimomannu tower. The 320th Bomb Group flew between 1 November 1943 and 21 September 1944 missions from Decimomannu air base on the Sardinia island. A red heart is painted against the white nose wheel covering. Most of the nose section had been repainted. No nickname had been applied, but a total of 86 mission markings. The name *Hubb* had been painted on the engine cowling. Many of the 12th Air Force B-26s had at least one of Browning M-2 from the gun package removed, in this case the lower machine gun. (USAF via Steve Birdsall)

B-26 B-15-MA

A total of 100 B-26 B-15-MA aircraft were built (41-31573 through 41-31672) under contract DA-46. Compared with the previous B-26 B-10-MA, only a few modifications had been introduced. The cockpit windshield was equipped with two windshield wipers, one for the pilot and one for the co-pilot. In addition, the oval window in the Plexiglas nose also received a windshield wiper. The windshield wipers in front of the cockpit windshield were generally disliked by the pilots, however, and quite frequently removed, so that only the pin shaped transmission shaft above the windshield remained. The windshield wiper became so unpopular that Martin deleted it with the beginning of the B-26 B-30-MA on the production line at Middle River.

The windshield wiper on the Plexiglas nose proved more popular among bombardiers and remained in most cases on the aircraft. There were some cases, however, of bombardiers removing that windshield wiper from the aircraft. The windshield wiper on the Plexiglas nose remained on the aircraft until the end of the Marauder production.

A hatch for the life raft was introduced to the top of the fuselage. This hatch was offset to the port and fitted with a handle on the outer surface. This hatch had been previously mounted on some of the previous B-26 B-10-MA block as well.

A distinctive feature that distinguished a B-26 B-15-MA from the previous B-10 block was the introduction of a short enforcement rib mounted on the wing leading edge

The 387th Bomb Group was almost exclusively equipped with the B-26 B-15-MA, when the unit crossed the Atlantic on the Northern Ferry Route and arrived at its base Station 162 Chipping Ongar during late June 1943. The 387th Bomb Group became the first Marauder unit without losses during the Atlantic crossing. In contrast to the first groups that went overseas in October 1942, the armament was retained for the ocean crossing, the barrels of the Browning M-2 machine guns being covered by protective material. *Bat Outa Hell II* was the personal aircraft of the Group Commander Colonel Carl R. Storrie. This B-26 B-15-MA (41-31643) subsequently received the unit code KX-Q and was allocated to the 558th Bomb Squadron. This particular Marauder flew its first mission, a diversion sortie near Dunkirk, on 31 July 1943. *Bat Outa Hell II* was transferred to the 323rd Bomb Group at Earls Colne after having flown 25 missions with the 387th Bomb Group and survived the war. (via Alan Crouchman)

Window Wiper / Hatch Development

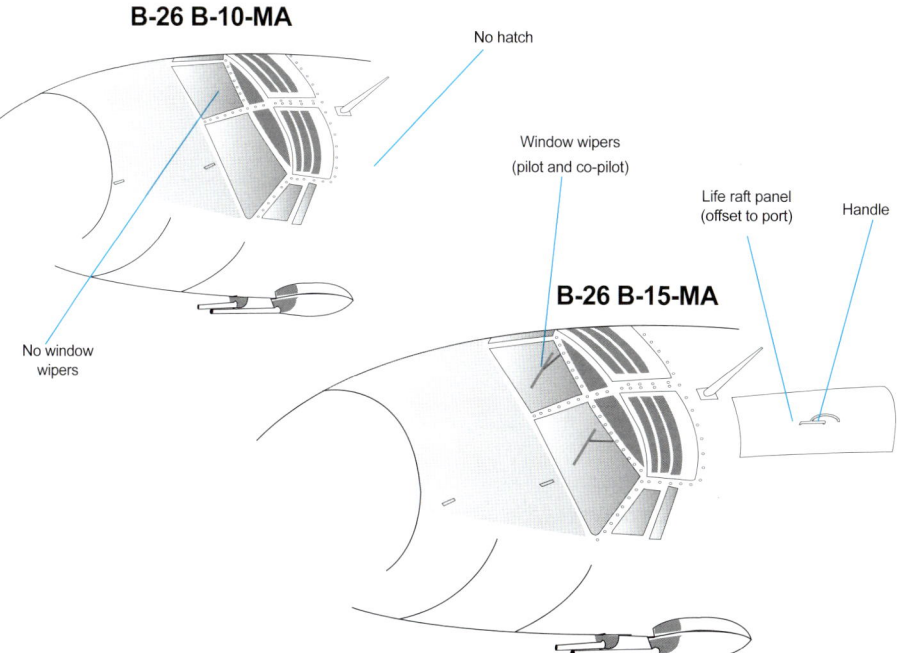

between the fuselage and the engine cowling. This rib was longer on the B-26 B-10-MA.

The B-26 B-15-MA had introduced on both sides of the rear fuselage an antenna cable that ran from the leading edge of the horizontal stabilizer to a small antenna mast on the rear fuselage below the turret. This arrangement of the antenna cable was directly taken over from the Marauder I of the Royal Air Force. These antenna cables were connected with the SCR-287 liaison radio.

An internal departure from the previous B-26 B-10-MA was the elimination of the fixed oxygen system, which was not necessary in an aircraft normally operating below 12,000 feet. In addition, the B-26 B-15-MA was equipped with the SCR-595A Identification of Friend from Foe (IFF) system.

The B-26 B-15-MA was delivered to the three Groups of the 12th Air Force operating in the Mediterranean Theater of operation to make up for attrition. The 386th and 387th Bomb Group brought Marauders of this block overseas when both units transferred from the United States to see combat with the 8th Air Force. Both formations arrived in England during June 1943 and their Marauders underwent modifications for specific 8th Air Force needs as had the B-26 B-10-MA. There were several instances of gun barrels breaking the Plexiglas at maximum depression. To prevent this damage, a modification order was issued in July 1943 to be carried out at 8th Air Force combat bases of the Marauder. It consisted of a simple wood stop on the gun mount restricting the downward movement of the guns.

Hell's Fury (41-31625) YA-R serves the 386th BG, 555th BS. The B-26 B-15-MA is the first block to have wipers on the cockpit window and the oval window in the Plexiglas nose. The fixed Browning M-2 machine gun in the starboard nose was standard on this batch.

Mississippi Mudcat, a B-26 B-15-MA (41-31657) TQ-W of the 387th BG, 559th BS, has been stripped of the fixed Browning .50-caliber machine gun, and of the windshield wipers on the cockpit and the window in the Plexiglas nose. (Alan Crouchman collection)

Jabbo Sky King the 2nd belonged to the 319th Bomb Group, 439th Bomb Squadron and had accomplished 37 missions by July 1943. The Marauder is credited with the destruction of seven Luftwaffe and one Italian aircraft. The B-26 B-15-MA (41-31609) was flown back to the United States for a War Bond selling tour. (GLMMAM)

Windshield Wiper – Nose Compartment

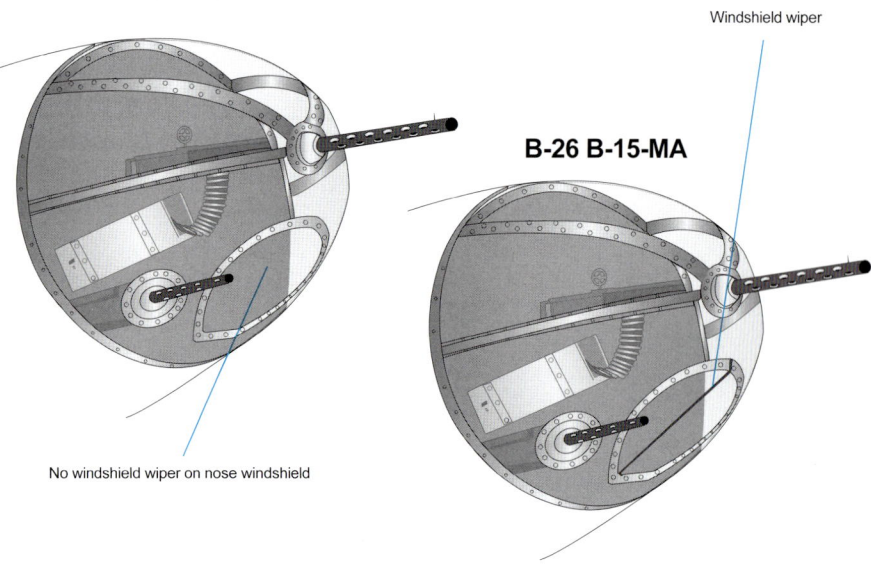

Rat Poison belonged to the original equipment of the 386th Bomb Group, 553rd Bomb Squadron. This B-26 B-15-MA (41-31606) AN-S came in June 1943 overseas without the white rectangle on both sides of American national marking. The rectangles and the red outlining of the national markings were introduced in late June 1943. *Rat Poison* carries the short lived Red outlining of the national marking. (USAF via Steve Birdsall)

D-Day stripes still remain on the lower rear fuselage of the veteran B-26 B-15-MA (41-31606) *Rat Poison*, seen here at A-60 Beaumont-sur-Oise air base in France. Under an order issued on 14 August 1943, the 164-mission veteran had replaced the red outline of the national marking with blue. Group identification bands were introduced to Marauder units in October 1943, shortly after the four B-26 groups were transferred to the 9th Air Force. The 386th Bomb Group wore a Yellow fin stripe on the tail. (Harry Holmes)

This B-26 B-15-MA (41-31642) awaits delivery at the ramp of Glenn L. Martin Company's Little River plant on 17 March 1943. The aircraft still wears the early-war version of the U.S. national markings. The addition of a white rectangle to each side of the star insignia was ordered on 28 June 1943, but just weeks before that date, on 12 June 1943, this aircraft crashed near Prestwick, Scotland, during its delivery flight on the Northern ferry route. (GLMMAM)

Loretta Young was a B-26 B-15-MA (41-31624) that had been allocated with the unit marking YA-S to the 386th Bomb Group, 555th Bomb Squadron. The veteran accomplished 65 missions before an ill-fated take off on 20 May 1944 from Station 164 Great Dunmow ended its career. The actress Loretta Young had autographed the nose of this Marauder before the group went overseas. (Steve Birdsall Collection)

B-26 B-20-MA

The B-26 B-20-MA became the first variant of the Marauder to be equipped with the electro-hydraulically powered Bell M-6 tail turret, with its clear Plexiglas section through which the machine gun barrel protruded. The tail window of the B-26 B-20-MA was now redesigned as a single piece. In contrast to the manually operated tail gun station, the one-piece tail canopy could be raised to provide access to the guns.

In the manually operated turret, spent shell casings fell into a small compartment under the guns and were cleared out after the aircraft had returned to base. On the Bell M-6, the spent cases and links were ejected from the underside of the turret though an aperture on the lower rear tail, around which a small fairing was fitted. Such spent cases could, however, be a hazard to Marauders flying lower in the same formation. An ejected .50-caliber case could easily smash trough Plexiglas. While the 8th and 9th Air Force did not consider such cases a threat, the 12th Air Force quickly adopted tail shell-case collectors that were mounted on the lower tail section of the B-26 as a field modification. No tail shell-case collectors were ever introduced on the production line of the B-model of the Marauder. The only unit to introduce field manufactured tail shell-case collectors in the 9th Air Force was the 344th Bomb Group. However, these collectors were considerably smaller than those used by the 12th Air Force. Output of the B-26 B-20-MA started in March 1943 and a total of 100 aircraft (41-31673 through 41-31772) were built.

Lead by B-26 B-20-MA (41-31739) DR-P, *The Old Vet*, 322nd Bomb Group Marauders warm up their engines at Station 485 at Andrews Field near Braintree. *Old Vet* survived to be scrapped at the ex-Luftwaffe base R-78 Landsberg in Bavaria. (Harry Holmes)

This B-26 B-20-MA (41-31707) KS-R *Five by Fives* belonging to the 387th Bomb Group, 557th Bomb Squadron accomplished 188 missions without a turn back. (Karl Berry via Alan Crouchman)

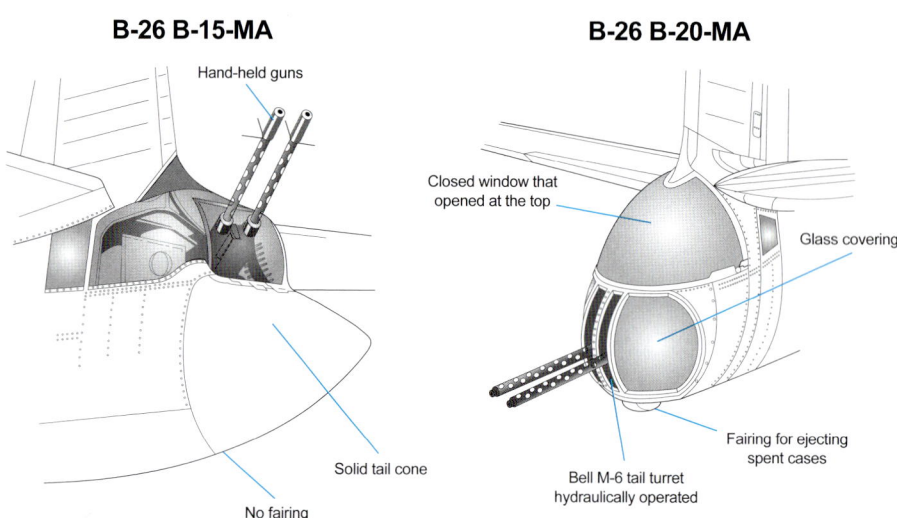

B-26 B-25-MA

The B-26 B-25-MA became the first Marauder variant to be equipped with additional armor protection for the pilot. Two rectangular armor plates were riveted against the skin around the cockpit compartment. Only the pilot sitting on the left seat benefitted from this additional armor protection; no armor plates were ever mounted on starboard where the co-pilot was located. With the introduction of the armor protection, the retractable circular air ventilator on the port side was deleted, but this device remained on starboard. A total of 100 B-26 B-25-MAs built: serial numbers 41-31773 trough 41-31872.

Two history-making Marauders belonged to the Block 25. *Mild and Bitter* (41-31819) and *Flak Bait* (41-31773) were both assigned to 322nd Bomb Group, which was based at the time of arrival of these two planes at Station 485 at Andrews Field in Essex. *Mild and Bitter* received much press coverage, since this particular Marauder flew its 99th and 100th mission on 9 May 1944 – the first British-based Marauder to do so. It flew all of its 100 missions on the original pair of Pratt & Whitney R-2800-43 Double Wasp engines and none of the missions were aborted due to technical reasons. A bitter fact for the *Mild and Bitter* was the success of B-26 B-10-MA (41-18322) *Hells Belle II* of the 319th Bomb Group in becoming the very first Marauder to complete 100 missions. *Hells Belle II* beat out *Mild and Bitter* by only eight days.

Glenn Luther Martin – the founder of the Glenn L. Martin Company – is surrounded on 25 September 1943 by its baseball team "Bombers." The B-26 B-25-MA (41-31822), nicknamed *The Marauder* serves as a backdrop. Most unusual for autumn 1943, this Marauder lacked any camouflage. Until late January 1944, all B-26s were delivered in olive drab to the Army Air Corps. *The Marauder* had the national markings red outlined and its serial number applied in black on the tail fin. (Lockheed Martin)

Mild and Bitter, a B-26 B-25-MA (41-31819) assigned with the unit marking DR-X to the 322nd Bomb Group, 452nd Bomb Squadron, flew all its 100 missions on its original Pratt & Whitney R-2800-43 Double Wasp engines and never aborted due to a technical failure. The magic mark was passed on 9 May 1944, when *Mild and Bitter* attacked a Luftwaffe airbase at Évreux near Rouen in Northern France. (GLMMAM)

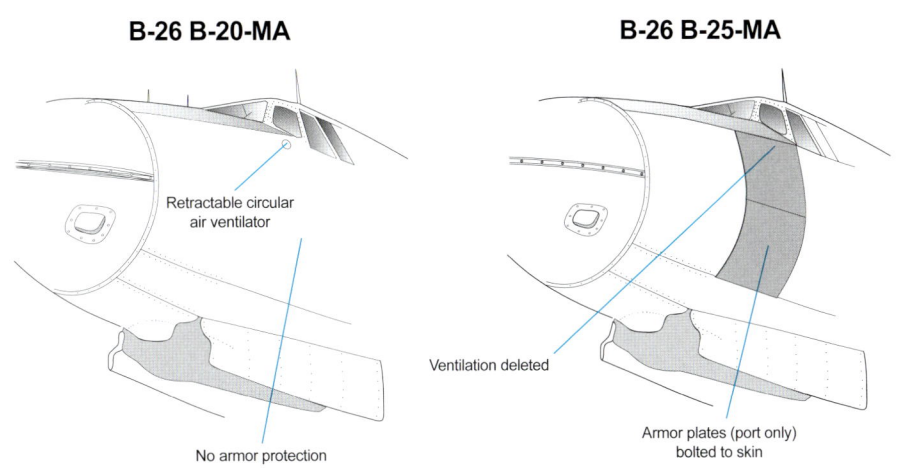

B-26 Flak Bait

The B-26 B-25-MA (41-31773) *Flak Bait*, belonging as PN-O to the 322nd Bomb Group, 449th Bomb Squadron, became the only Allied aircraft in World War II to surpass the 200 mission mark. Its first pilot, Lieutenant James J. Farrell, also chose the plane's nickname. *Flak Bait* flew its first mission on 16 August 1943. 1st Lieutenant Horace C. Rodgers took it out on its 100th mission on 1 June 1944. Over the course of its operation, *Flak Bait* was progressively modified. The aircraft received a silver shark-tooth-shaped tab on each wing tip. The two original Pitot tubes with a vane on top of the boom were replaced by a pair of flush Pitot tubes worn on the B-26 G models. The windshield wipers on the cockpit windshield and the Plexiglas nose were all deleted.

To celebrate its 200th mission, *Flak Bait* acted on 18 April 1945 as a lead ship for the entire 322nd Bomb Group. After return to A-89 Le Culot home base in Belgium, a large bomb was painted onto the mission board of *Flak Bait*. The plane's assigned pilot, Lieutenant Warren Langar, took *Flak Bait* on its 202nd and last mission – to an oil depot at Schrobenhausen near Neuburg an der Donau airbase in Bavaria – on 24 April 1945.

After the end of the war, the image marking the 200th mission was moved to a place under the score board. While based in occupied Germany, *Flak Bait*'s port Pratt & Whitney R-2800-43 Double Wasp engine was replaced with the entire cowling of a silver Marauder. Unlike the other B-26s of the 322nd Bomb Group, *Flak Bait* was not flown to Landsberg air depot for demolition, but was retained as a transport hawk.

Today the front section of this historic B-26 is on exhibit at the National Air and Space Museum at Washington D.C.

Flak Bait flew more missions than any other Allied bomber in World War II. This B-26 B-25-MA (41-31773) accomplished a total of 202 missions with the 322nd Bomb Group. After completing its 200th mission on 18 April 1945 against strong points at Magdeburg (Central Germany) a large bomb was painted into the mission board. Since *Flak Bait* flew as a lead ship for the 322nd Bomb Group on its 200th mission, no flexible machine gun was carried in the nose. The crew names were painted on the nose and below the cockpit glazing. (Jay P. Spenser)

Celebrating its 200th mission, *Flak Bait* serves as a lead ship for the entire 322nd Bomb Group on 18 April 1945. Captain William G. Fort took the veteran to the target, a marshalling yard at Magdeburg in central Germany. (USAF)

The 200 bomb symbol had been relocated to a position under the mission board and the word "missions" now omitted in the bomb symbol. The crew names were deleted from the nose and the cockpit section of *Flak Bait*. (Martin Kyburz/Swiss Mustangs)

B-26 B-30-MA

A total of 100 B-26 B-30-MA (41-31873 through 41-31972) aircraft were built as part of the Army Air Corps Contract DA-46. The B-26 B-30-MA differed from the preceding Block 25 in that the two windshield wipers were now deleted from the cockpit windshield on the production line at Middle River. The windshield wipers for the pilot and co-pilot were generally disliked and many crew chiefs had removed these items from the aircraft as a field modification.

At about the time the B-26 B-30-MA reached England, the four B-26 units (322nd, 323rd, 386th, and 387th Bomb Group) belonging to the 3rd Bomb Wing of the 8th Air Force were transferred to the 9th Air Force, charged with building up tactical air power for the Allied invasion of occupied Europe. This transfer took place on 16 October 1943. Between 14 May and 9 October 1943 the Marauders flew more than 4,000 sorties for the 8th Air Force with a marginal loss rate of only 0.3 percent.

The four bomb groups retained the same bases in England, and the same squadron markings. However, the 9th Air Force introduced a system of group identification markings that became effective shortly after the Marauder joined the 9th Air Force. Bomb Groups were to be distinguished by different colored horizontal fin stripes. No stripe was carried by the 322nd Bomb Group. The 323rd Bomb Group wore a white stripe, the 386th Bomb Group sported a yellow one, and a black-yellow stripe became the marking of the 387th Bomb Group.

Booger Red II had the fixed Browning M-2 machine gun removed and the aperture faired over with a piece of Plexiglas. A measure quite often adopted by English based Marauder units. No armor plates were ever applied on the starboard cockpit section. This B-26 B-30-MA (41-31874) had the nickname and the mission markings applied on both sides of the nose. *Booger Red II* was the second production B-26 of Block 30. (Bob Allen via Alan Crouchman)

Bar Fly carries the Yellow Group marking on the tail fin, which identifies this B-26 B-30-MA (41-31877) as belonging to the 386th Bomb Group. Most unusual for 9th Air Force Marauders, the lower Browning M-2 in the gun package had been deleted. *Bar Fly* crashed on its 176th mission with Lt. Donald C. Altenburger at the controls on 1 January 1945 after an engine failure during take off at A-60 Beaumont-sur-Oise airfield in France. For a long time, this Marauder with the unit marking RU-V held the record for the B-26 with most missions and flew its 100th mission in early July 1944. (Harry Holmes.)

Booger Red II flew a total of 132 missions with the 387th Bomb Group, 559th Bomb Squadron. The Marauder with the unit marking TQ-O suffered severe damage in an attack of Luftwaffe Messerschmitt Bf 109 Gs on 23 December 1944, but limped back to base at A-71 Clastres in France only to be salvaged there. *Booger Red II* flew the first mission on 14 September 1943 to Lille airfield in Northern France with its original pilot Lieutenant Jack Skipper. (Alan Crouchman)

B-26 B-35 to B-50-MA

The B-26 B-35-MA was the first production block to be equipped with an alcohol carburetor de-icer system, which proved in operation quite troublesome to handle. Externally this block was identical to the B-26 B-30-MA and in all, a total of 100 aircraft were built (41-31973 through 41-32072).

The B-26 B-40-MA saw the re-introduction of the long stabilization rib on the wing leading edge between the fuselage and the engine cowling. A distinctive feature of Marauders built in Baltimore was a uniquely shaped piece of armor that served as a cover panel for the drift meter bracket on the port side of the nose. A square plate covered the drift meter bracket on B-26 Cs manufactured in Omaha. Since the rear bomb bay was seldom used by 9th and 12th Air Force, these bomb bay doors were deleted from these and all forthcoming production blocks of the Marauder. A total of 101 B-26 B-40-MA aircraft were built under contract DA-1049 (42-43260 through 42-43357 and 42-43360 to 42-43361 and 42-43459). The 320th Bomb Group started putting two additional slot-shaped inlets on top of each engine cowling as a field modification. This unique modification by the 320th Bomb Group was done on a few late B models of the Marauder. A single B-26 B-40-MA (42-43319) was factory modified with a square shaped waist window on each side. In addition, an L-shaped Pitot tube was introduced under the port wing, instead of the two Pitot tubes located on the outer wing leading edge on standard production B-26 B-40-MAs. These modifications were never introduced in the production line of the Marauder but, beginning with the Block B-55-MA, the L-shaped Pitot tube was introduced on the lower nose section.

The B-26 B-45-MA became the first Marauder variant to be equipped with a direct-vision panel on the port windscreen. This panel resulted in the addition of a diagonal brace in the windshield. No direct-vision panel or brace was ever introduced on the co-pilot side. The lower portion of the direct-vision panel could be hinged up in order to give the pilot an unobstructed view in icing conditions. The B-26 B-45-MA saw the introduction of the SCR-695 IFF device and the SCR-522 VHF command radio set.

Martin started to fit on the production line specific equipment for late production B-26 Bs, that would be sent to the 12th Air Force in the Mediterranean Theater of Operation (MTO). This equipment included a sickle-shaped antenna that was located close to the antenna mast and offset to the port atop of cockpit. Another dedicated 12th Air Force feature was the introduction of a centerline-mounted antenna on the rear lower fuselage. In all, 91 B-26 B-45-MA aircraft were built (42-95738 through 42-95828) under contract AC-31733. The first examples rolled off the assembly line in Baltimore in November 1943.

The B-26 B-50-MA was externally identical to the B-26 B-45-MA and, in all, a total of 200 of the aircraft were built (42-95829 through 42-96028). Most B-26 B-50-MAs had a medium green applied over the dark olive drab on wing surfaces and the tail fin to soften the edges of tailplane and wings. This pattern was applied on the production line. The B-26 B-50-MA became the last block of completely camouflaged aircraft built in Baltimore.

Marauders - 9th and 12th Air Forces

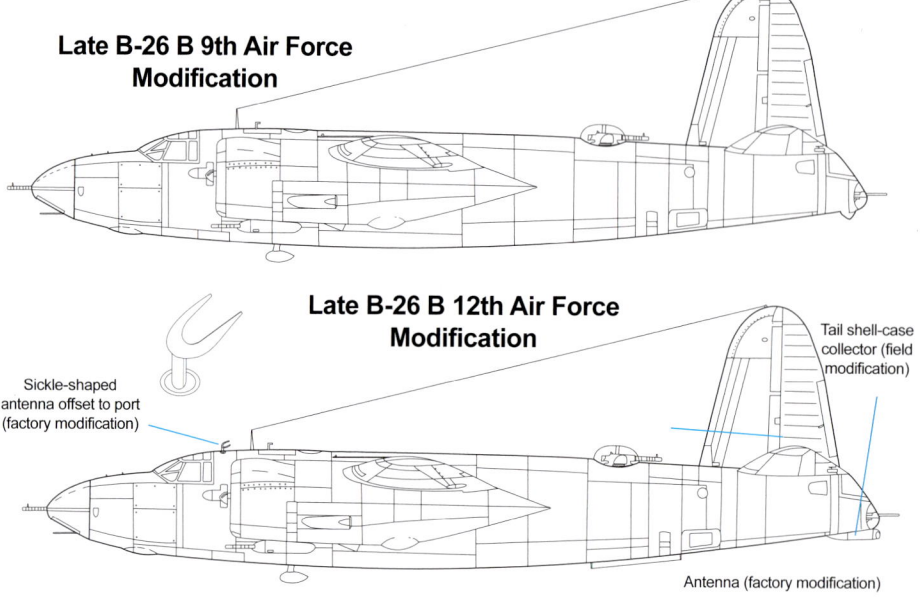

The shark mouth became the squadron marking for the 444th Bomb Squadron, 320th Bomb Group. The two slot-shaped inlets behind the engine cowlings are a field modification that had been introduced on some few 320th Bomb Group Marauders. Non standard at all for Baltimore built B-26 Bs is the small slanted antenna mast on top of the fuselage, close to the wing root. This is a feature only seen on Omaha-built B-26 Cs. The *Marlin* is a B-26 B-40-MA (42-43304). (Harry Holmes)

This Marauder assigned to the 12th Air Force had introduced the tall two digit Battle Number during October 1943. The Yellow number identifies the 320th Bomb Group. Medium green had been painted over the dark olive drab on wing surfaces and the tail fin to soften the edges. This B-26 B-50-MA (42-95991) was written off after a crash landing at Decimomannu air base on 19 August 1944 after the 320th Bomb Group had attacked road bridges South of Embrun in France. (Steve Birdsall)

This brand new Martin B-26 B-45-MA (42-95739) has 12th Air Force specific equipment fitted on the production line, such as the sickle-shaped antenna on top of the cockpit and the centerline-mounted antenna on the rear lower fuselage. Neither of these types of antenna was never carried on B-26 Bs manufactured for the 9th Air Force. This particular Marauder was allocated to the 17th Bomb Group, 37th Bomb Squadron, with the Battle Number 34 issued in red on the tail fin. (GLMMAM)

With the exception of the tailplane, factory-applied camouflage has been taken off the vertical stabilizer and upper surfaces of this B-26 B-50-MA (42-95899). A distinctive field modification of the 344th Bomb Group, 9th Air Force, is the small tail shell-case collector mounted on the lower tail of this Marauder. In sharp contrast to the 12th Air Force, those B-26 B/Cs assigned to the 9th Air Force were with the exception of the 344th Bomb Group not equipped with a tail shell-case collector. The tail and horizontal surfaces were painted in medium green and dark olive drab, which was a standard procedure for this block. The unit code N3-P identifies this B-26 B-50-MA as belonging to the 344th Bomb Group, 496th Bomb Squadron. (Jerry Scutts via Eddie J. Creek)

Nose Development

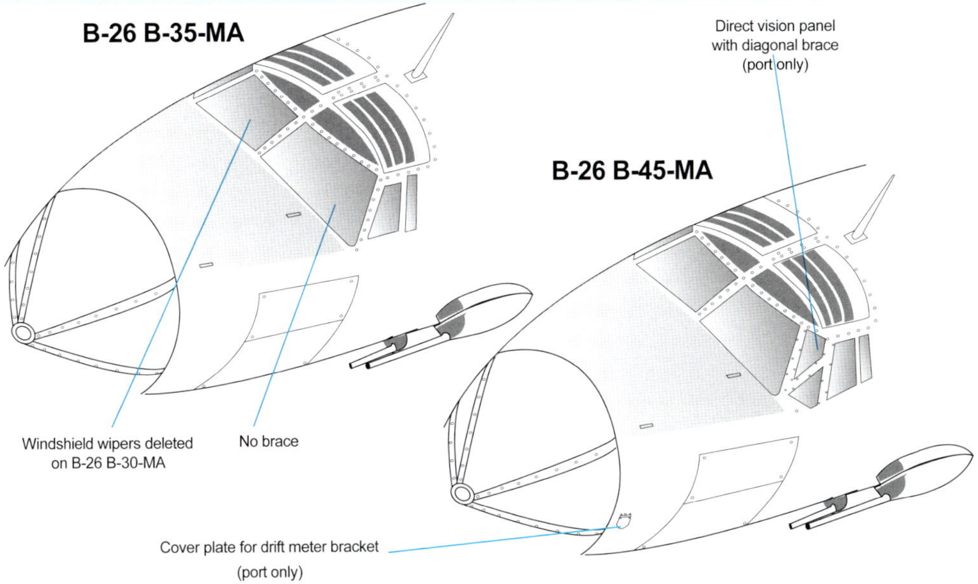

B-26 B-35-MA

B-26 B-45-MA

Direct vision panel with diagonal brace (port only)

Windshield wipers deleted on B-26 B-30-MA

No brace

Cover plate for drift meter bracket (port only)

33

B-26 B-55-MA

The B-26 B-55-MA became the last block of the B-variant to be built. Compared with the previous B-26 B-50-MA a number of modifications had been introduced. The most significant was the deletion of the two Pitot tubes on the leading edge of each wing. Their place an L-shaped Pitot tube was mounted on the centerline in front of the nose wheel bay.

The front pin shaped aiming device on the nose was relocated to the rear. The fixed Browing M-2 machine gun in the bombardier's compartment was deleted on the production line. Previously, many Bomb Groups in the 9th and 12th Air Force had deleted the fixed machine gun as a field modification. Although the manufacturer deleted the gun, no corresponding change was made to the Plexiglas nose, and the oval aperture remained through the production cycle of the B-variant. This aperture was faired over with another piece of oval shaped Plexiglas and fixed with bolts.

All B-26 B-55-MA aircraft were delivered from the production line at Middle River without a shark-tooth-shaped tab on the rear of the wing tips. This kind of a tab was introduced on a number of B-26 B-55-MAs as a field modification. In contrast to the Baltimore-built B-26 Bs that all lacked this device, the shark-tooth-shaped tab became

The *Big Hairy Bird* belonged to the 397th Bomb Group, 599th Bomb Squadron and carried the unit code 6B-T. The lack of the Pitot tubes on both wing leading edge became a typical feature of the B-26 B-55-MA. Like most silver Marauder of the 9th Air Force has the *Big Hairy Bird* the Group marking on tail large black outlined. This B-26 B-55-MA (42-96165) was transferred after the war to the 387th Bomb Group, 558th Bomb Squadron and adopted the new unit code KX-T. (Harry Holmes)

standard on the production line of the Omaha-built Marauders, beginning with the Block C-25-MO.

The Norden M-7 gyroscopic bombsight replaced the D-8 bombsight in this block.

The first 101 B-26 B-55-MAs were delivered with camouflage consisting of dark olive drab with medium green on the upper surfaces to be used to soften the edges of tailplanes and wings. The lower part of the airframe was painted in medium green. By the end of January 1944 all B-26 B-55-MA manufactured at Baltimore were delivered without any camouflage in bare aluminum silver. The first example of a total of 99 aircraft of this block leaving the Baltimore production line unpainted was aircraft 42-96129. Only the anti glare panels in front of the cockpit section and on the inner engine cowlings remained in olive drab. The serial number on the tail was applied in Black on silver aircraft. The 9th Air Force changed the three letter unit code on the rear fuselage from light gray to black. The 323rd and 386th Bomb Group outlined its horizontal fin stripe in black, and the 394th and 397th Bomb Groups outlined the vertical stripe on the tail fin as well. The 344th and 391st Bomb Group outlined the triangle on their silver B-26s. The Marauder units of the 12th Air Force outlined the tall Battle Number in thin Black.

A total of 200 examples of the final variant of the B-26 B were produced (42-96029 through 42-96228). The last B-26 B-55-MA rolled off the assembly line in February 1944. A total of 1,983 examples of the B-model were been built between May 1942 and February 1944 on the two assembly lines at Baltimore, resulting in an average monthly output of 94 aircraft.

B-26 B-55-MA Development

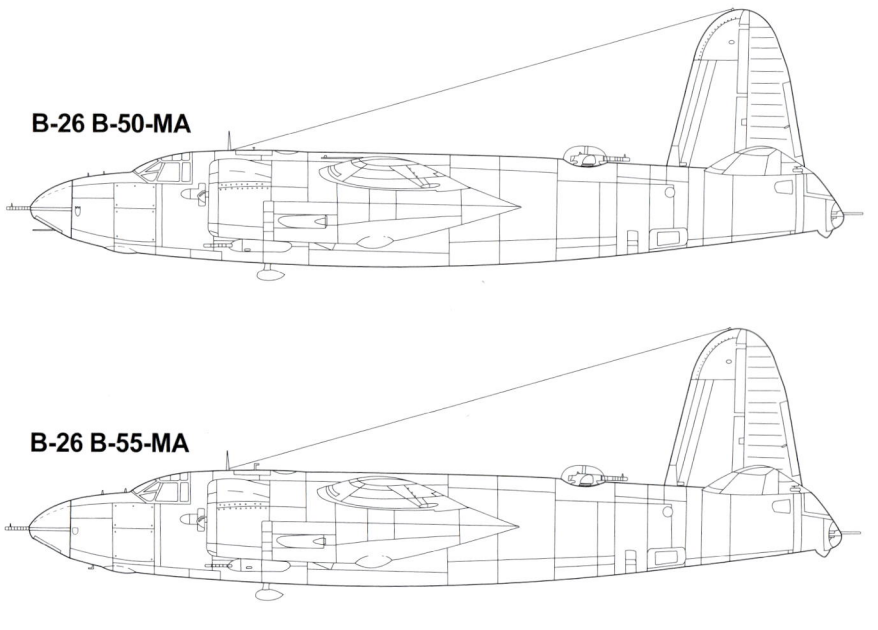

An all silver fleet of 397th Bomb Group Marauders flies low over the English countryside in April 1944 before the D-Day stripes were applied on the aircraft. The first silver B-26 B-55-MA left the assembly line in January 1944. Most 9th Air Force units had on silver B-26s the unit marking on the tail fin large Black outlined. Nearest the camera is 42-96137 with the unit code 9F-Y, which was listed as salvaged on 15 May 1944. This Marauder is followed by 42-96191 (9F-N), which subsequently adopted the nickname *The Milk Run Special*. The 397th Bomb Group became the first Marauder unit of the Army Air Corps to be equipped with entirely silver aircraft. (Harry Holmes)

Little Lady suffered a crash landing on 24 February 1945 at its home base A-72 Péronne in France. With the unit marking X2-O, this B-26 B-55-MA (42-96154) belonged to the 397th Bomb Group, 596th Bomb Squadron. A dedicated feature of the B-26 B-55-MA block is the absence of a Pitot tube on both wing tips. The shark-tooth tab on the wing tip is a field modification. The upper black-white invasion stripes were overpainted in olive drab on the fuselage. (Alain Pelletier)

Milk Run Special – once belonging to the 397th Bomb Group – was transferred after the war with the unit marking TQ-M to the 387th Bomb Group, 559th Bomb Squadron. The lower part of the 397th Bomb Group marking remained on the tail plane. This B-26 B-55-MA suffered a blown tire on 26 June 1945. (F. Krumenacher via Alan Crouchman)

Wing Tip Development

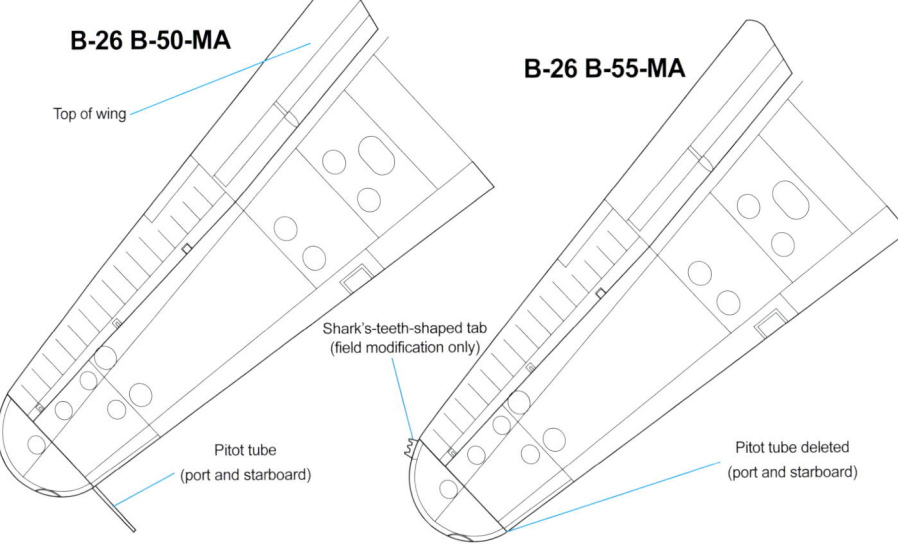

35

Omaha built B-26 C

The Glenn L. Martin Company had orders from the Army Air Corps for nearly 1,000 of the B-26s by late September 1940. This huge order for Marauders was well beyond the capacities of the Martin factory at Middle River in Baltimore. Anticipating a war, the United States administration started planning government owned plants for fighter and bomber aircraft. One such huge plant was erected south of Omaha, the largest city of Nebraska. Omaha was chosen as a site for bomber production because of its location deep inside the United States.

A contract was signed on 14 February 1941 awarding to the Glenn L. Martin Company the right to operate the plant, which was located near the rural community of Bellevue on the area of Offutt air field. Glenn Luther Martin created for this purpose the Glenn L. Martin Nebraska Company. By March 1941, the company had a letter of intent from the government to build 1,200 B-26s at the Omaha plant. In parallel, the Ford Motor Company was provided with a license to build the Pratt & Whitney R-2800-43 Double Wasp powerplant at an newly erected factory in Dearborn, Michigan. The first Ford built Double Wasp was flight tested for the first time on 14 February 1942 in a Marauder. All B-26 C aircraft built in Omaha were powered by the Pratt & Whitney R-2800-43 engine.

The firm order for these 1,200 B-26 Cs was placed on 28 June 1941 under the contract AC-19342, and amounted to $162,475,685.40. The B-26 C became essentially a copy of the B-26 B built at Baltimore. Full production of the B-26 C began on 8 June 1942. Various sub contractors furnished assemblies for the B-26 C to be assembled at Omaha. The wings as well the horizontal and vertical stabilizers were manufactured by Goodyear, the front and middle segment of the fuselage was furnished by Chrysler and the rear fuselage section built by Hudson.

Labor available in Omaha consisted mainly of farm workers, housewives, and meat packinghouse workers. At the time when Marauder production was launched, a total of 8,500 employees worked for the Glenn L. Martin Nebraska Company. When Marauder production was at its peak, there were 11,019 persons employed, with more than 40 percent of the workforce being women. The plant was like a small city with its own telephone system, bank, post office, hotel, library, and police and fire systems.

B-26 C-5 to C-30-MO

The first three B-26 C-5-MOs were accepted by the Army Air Corps in August 1942 and a total of 86 Marauders were accepted by the end of 1942. Work in Omaha went on in two shifts, six days a week, with Sunday remaining a day off. These B-26 C-5-MOs were in fact the first Marauders to be equipped with the long wing and tall tail – a remarkable five months before this modification was adopted at the Martin factory at Baltimore. No short-wing B-26s were ever built at Omaha. These early B-26 C-5-MOs differed from the Baltimore built B-26 B-10-MAs in having a tail bumper on the lower rear fuselage and the small carburetor air intakes on the engine cowlings. However, most production B-26 C-5-MOs had the large carburetor intakes and no tail bumper. These early B-26 C-5-MOs were equipped with the small, 47-inch main wheel tires and lacked the bulge in the main wheel doors. The first Omaha-built Marauders lacked the circular window on the rear fuselage that subsequently became standard on the B-26 C-5-MO. However, most B-26 C-5-MOs received two circular rear observation windows on the production line at Omaha, while the contemporary B-26 B-10-MA model always carried a single circular observation window. The first few B-26 C-5-MOs went overseas to the European Theater of Operation with the 449th and 451st Bomb Squadron of the 322nd Bomb Group and arrived in May 1943 at Bury St. Edmunds. These Omaha-built Marauders were modified to 8th Air Force requirement upon arrival as were the Baltimore-built B-26 Bs. There were a total of 115 B-26 C-5-MO built (Serial Number 41-34673 through 41-34680, 41-34682 through 41-34686, 41-34688, 41-34694, 41-34696 through 41-34701, 41-34743 through 41-34776, 41-34788 through 41-34847).

The B-26 C-6-MO became a ground attack derivative of the Marauder with the co-pilot's seat and control column omitted and a lightweight seat substituted so that the navigator could operate flaps and undercarriage controls during take-off and landing. An escape and entrance hatch was on the lower fuselage just aft the gun package. Like the B-26 C-5-MO, the B-26 C-6-MO was equipped with two circular observation windows on the rear fuselage as a modification-center feature. The first B-26 C-6-MO went overseas as an original assignment of 323rd Bomb Group and arrived in May 1943 at Station 119 at Horham (Suffolk) in the United Kingdom. However, these aircraft were never used for its intended purpose, but instead like the B-26 C-5-MOs of this unit in conventional bombing. There were a total of 60 B-26 C-6-MO built (Serial Number

This B-26 C-5-MO (41-34685) was one of the first Marauder that left the assembly lines of the Glenn L. Martin Nebraska Company at Omaha. The two circular observation windows on the rear fuselage are a typical feature of Omaha-built Marauders, while Baltimore built B-26s had a single observation window. The tail bumper was mounted on early examples of the B-26 C-5-MO only. (GLMMAM)

41-34681, 41-34687, 41-34689 through 41-34693, 41-34695, 41-34702 through 41-34742, 41-34777 through 41-34787).

The B-26 C-10-MO saw the introduction of windshield wipers on the cockpit window and the Plexiglas nose. Two rectangular armor plates were mounted on the port cockpit section. This block also had two windshield deflectors mounted in front of each waist position. As on the B-26 B-10-MA, there was a single circular window on both sides of the rear fuselage and there was no tail bumper. The B-26 C-10-MO became the first version to be equipped with the Bell M-6 tail turret. This variant had adopted the escape and entrance hatch on the lower fuselage of the B-26 C-6-MO. The first B-26 C-10-MA arrived in the United Kingdom with the 323rd Bomb Group in May 1943 and a month later with the 386th Bomb Group. A total of 60 Marauders of this block were built (Serial Number 41-34848 through 41-34907), the first examples left the assembly line in March 1943.

The B-26 C-15-MO and B-26 C-20-MO remained externally identical to the B-26 C-10-MO, except for the deletion of the escape and entrance hatches from these models. There were a total of 90 B-26 C-15-MOs built (41-34908 through 41-34997) as well 175 B-26 C-20-MOs (Serial Number 41-34998 through 41-35172).

The Glenn L. Martin Nebraska Company not only copied the B-model of the Marauder but developed a number of improvements for its C model. The shark teeth-shaped tab on the rear wing was one such innovation. This tab was introduced for the first time on the B-26 C-25-MO and was subsequently adopted on the Baltimore production line for the first time on the B-26 G. A total of 199 B-26 C-25-MO aircraft were built (Serial Numbers 41-35173 through 41-35372). Three aircraft of this block were converted to the AT-23 advanced trainer standard.

The B-26 C-30-MO saw the introduction of the direct vision panel with the diagonal brace on the port windshield of the cockpit. On this variant the provisions for the external bomb rack were deleted and the rear bomb bay doors were faired over. In all a total of 177 B-26 C-30-MO were built (Serial Numbers 41-35374 through 41-35515, 41-35517 through 41-35551, and 41-35553 through 41-35560). A total of 104 aircraft of this block were manufactured for the Royal Air Force as the Marauder II, with RAF-specific equipment and a number of detail changes. A total of 48 aircraft from Block 30 were built as AT-23 trainers.

Yankee Guerrilla, a B-26 C-15-MO (41-34946) and the rest of the 386th Bomb Group leave Dover in England behind, *en route* to the Normandy beachheads on D-Day. The white-and-black invasion stripes were applied on fuselage and wings on 4 June 1944, two days before the start of the invasion on all 9th Air Force aircraft. Yankee Guerrilla carries the unit code YA-L of the 555th Bomb Squadron. This Marauder crashed at Rethondes, France, during a mission to Düren, Germany, on 5 October 1944. (Steve Birdsall)

This freshly completed B-26 C-25-MO (41-35289) is shown during an open house at the Glenn L. Martin Nebraska Company in Omaha on 4 June 1943. The fixed Browning 0.50-caliber machine guns have not yet been mounted in the fuselage fairings, but a dummy torpedo is mounted centerline on the lower fuselage. The Marauder left the assembly line in natural silver, with only the tail painted Olive Drab. It would receive its camouflage in a separate paint shop at the Glenn L. Martin Nebraska firm. (GLAMMAM)

Production of the B-26 C-6-MO is in full swing at Glenn L. Martin in Omaha, Nebraska, on 22 December 1943. The first three B-26 C-6s all went with the 323rd Bomb Group overseas. In the foreground is 41-34727, later allocated with the unit code VT-O to the 453rd Bomb Squadron and nicknamed *Ticklish Percy*. Ship 727 followed 41-34733 and 41-34734 on the production line. At its peak, 11,019 people were involved in B-26 C Marauder output. More than 40 percent of the work force were women. (GLMMAM)

Entrance Door Development

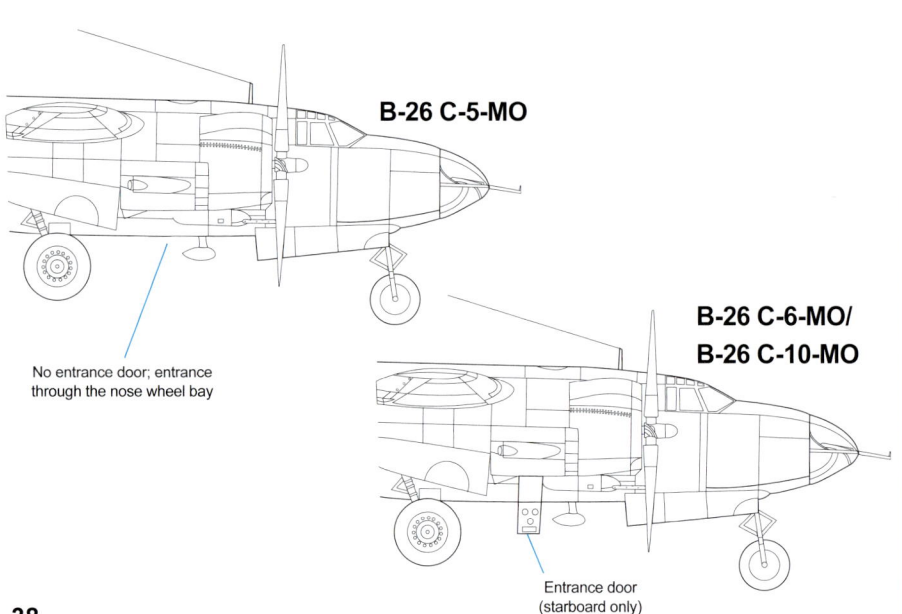

With the left engine gone and the propeller feathered, B-26 C-25-MO (41-35177) Battle Number 17 struggles to keep up with the 17th Bomb Group, 34th Bomb Squadron, by dropping ammunition belts to lighten the ship. German Flak defending a bridge at Roccasecca, Italy, damaged ship number 17 on 30 December 1943. (Harry Holmes)

Sexy Betsy drops its deadly load over a defended area at Argentan in France on 14 June 1944. This was the 208th mission for the Great Dunmow based 386th Bomb Group. *Sexy Betsy* was an Omaha built B-26 C-25-MO (41-35358). The unit marking YA-V denotes that this Marauder had belonged to the 555th Bomb Squadron. (Harry Holmes)

B-26 C-5-MO
No entrance door; entrance through the nose wheel bay

B-26 C-6-MO/
B-26 C-10-MO
Entrance door (starboard only)

The B-26 C-10-MO (Serial Number 41-34857) adopted the entrance hatch on the lower fuselage behind the package guns from the B-26 C-6-MO. *Jill Fitter* was accepted by the Army Air Corps on 28 March 1943 and was one of only two original 454th Bomb Squadron aircraft that had survived World War II. The battered veteran with the group marking RJ-O flew on the 323rd Bomb Group's final mission on 25 April 1945 against the Me 262 storage depot at Erding in Bavaria, accomplishing thereby its 195th mission – a figure only beaten by *Flak Bait*. *Jill Fitter* was flown to R-78 Landsberg air base in Bavaria where the B-26 was destroyed on 18 June 1945. (John R. Grimm)

Two Omaha-built Marauders belonging to the 323rd Bomb Group, 454th Bomb Squadron are *en route* to their target in occupied Europe on 6 December 1944. The invasion stripes have been overpainted with olive drab on both aircraft. The olive drab Marauder is a B-26 C-25-MO (41-35253) RJ-S and nicknamed *Black Magic IV*, while the silver ship is a B-26 C-45-MO (42-107614) RJ-H. *Lady Luck III* ran out of luck on 23 December 1944, when the crew had to bail out from the battle damaged B-26 C-45-MO. (Harry Holmes)

AT-23 B-MO

A total of 350 AT-23 B-MO aircraft were built as target tugs with the aim of providing gunners with high-altitude shooting trials. The AT-23 B-MO was based on the B-26 C of Block 35 and Block 40.

These target tugs differed from the standard production B-26 C in that the armament and the armor protection for the crew were deleted. A tail cone – similar to that of the early B-26 A-MA variants – faired over the missing Bell M-6 tail turret. The circular aperture of the Martin 250 CE turret in the upper rear fuselage was faired over as well.

The AT-23 B-MO was equipped with an electric cable winch and target carriers. Some 544 kilograms lighter than the combat B-26, the AT-23 B-MO was 40km/h faster.

The AT-23 B-MOs had the following serial numbers: 41-35371, 41-35373, 41-35516, 41-35539, 41-35541 through 41-35547, 41-35552, and 41-35561 through 41-35872. In addition, a total of 26 aircraft in the B-26 C-45-MO production block were converted to AT-23 B-MO standard, receiving the numbers 42-107471 through 42-107496. A large number of AT-23 B-MO aircraft were retrofitted with a vent mast to provide proper ventilation for the two main fuselage tanks. This vent mast was located centerline on the upper fuselage.

These AT-23 B-MOs were allocated to gunnery training units in the United States. A dozen AT-23 B-MOs went overseas in May 1944 and were based at Station 236 Toome in Northern Ireland as part of the 8th Air Force. These aircraft were used by bomber and fighter units for gunnery training remained in the U.K. until summer 1945.

This AT-23 B-MO (41-35295) became one of the first target tug built by the Glenn L. Martin Nebraska Company at Omaha. A total of three AT-23 B-MO were built in the Block 25. The target lacked all armament, instead of the Bell M-6 turret a conical tail had been introduced. The port engine cowling and the main wheel doors were obviously taken from another aircraft. (Harry Holmes)

B-26 C-45-MO

The B-26 C-45-MO was the last model of the Marauder to be built by the Glenn L. Martin Nebraska Company. Initially, the Army Air Corps contract AC-38728 issued on 15 July 1943 called for a total of 1,000 B-26 C-45-MOs. However, this order was sharply cut by 615 aircraft on 12 August 1943. The reason for the reduction in the order was the fact that the Army Air Corps had decided to build the huge Boeing B-29 Superfortress under license at Omaha.

Comprising 359 B-26 C-45-MOs (Serial Number 42-107497 through 42-107855) and 26 TB-23 B-MOs (42-107471 through 42-107496) this was by far the largest block ever built in the B-26 production cycle. This block was, however, the subject of constant improvements on the production line. As a result, the first examples of the B-26 C-45-MO were quite different than the last one built at Omaha. A Marauder of this block number was delivered at a cost of $78,677 each, which was nearly half the unit price of a Baltimore-built B-26 B-40-MA, which was priced at $156,215. The first 19 aircraft (Serial number 42-107497 through 42-107515) from this block were delivered to the Royal Air Force as Marauder IIs.

The B-26 C-45-MO was roughly comparable to the B-26 B-45-MA built at Baltimore. However, the B-26 C-45-MO differed in a number of details from the Baltimore-built Marauder. Instead of a square cover panel for the drift meter bracket on the port nose, the armor cover panel on the B-26 B was uniquely shaped. The B-26 B had – like the B-26 C-30-MO – two pin shaped aiming devices for the gun packs in front of the nose, the B-26 C-45-MO had three of them. The closest sight to the window was a ring sight and the middle pin shaped sight had a small strut to starboard.

Another distinctive feature of all Omaha-built B-26 C-45-MOs was the introduction of a small, left-slanted antenna mast on the port side of the upper fuselage, close to the wing root section. This antenna mast connected an antenna cable to the leading edge of the vertical stabilizer. A further feature of the Baltimore-built B-26 B was the introduction of an antenna on the lower centerline fuselage on B-26 C-45-MOs that left the production line at Omaha. On new B-models this antenna was only fitted on Marauders to be delivered to the 12th Air Force. This antenna also omitted from the factory fresh B-26 C-30-MOs that were bound for the 9th Air Force. The fixed Browning M-2 0.50-caliber machine gun was deleted from the nose section of the B-26 C-45-MO. The two windshield wipers were deleted from the cockpit windshield of the B-26 C-45-MO. A unique feature of the B-26 C-45-MO was the application of the Army Air Corps stenciling on the upper port armor plate. All other Marauder blocks built at Baltimore and Omaha had this stenciling located on top of the port nose. In contrast to the B-26 B-55-MA, the last batch built at Baltimore, all B-26 C-45-MOs retained the conventional Pitot tube configuration on the leading edge of both wings and did not adopt the L-shaped Pitot tube on the lower surface of the nose.

Early B-26 C-45-MOs took over the shark-tooth-shaped tab on the both wing tips, but the majority of this variant of the aircraft lacked these tabs. The first all-silver B-26 C-45-MOs were delivered in January 1944 and the main part of this block left the factory in natural silver. Since the production of the B-26 C-45-MO lasted two months longer than the manufacture of the last B-26 B variant at Baltimore, the last production examples of the B-26 B-45-MO received a ring for the tail gunner mounted on the port rear fuselage emergency exit hatch. This feature was introduced simultaneously on the B-26 F-1-MA at the Baltimore production line. This ring opened a fabric covered aperture in the hatch, that covered a handle for opening the door for the tail gunner from the outside. On previous Marauder models the door could only be opened from the inside.

The last B-26 C-45-MO left the assembly line at Omaha on 4 April 1944. A total of 1,585 B-26 Cs and AT-23 B-MOs had been built between August 1942 and April 1944 at Omaha, representing nearly a third of the total Marauder production.

The first Omaha-built B-29 Superfortress left the factory on 24 May 1944. When production finally ceased on 18 September 1945, a total of 531 B-29s had been built, including *Enola Gay* and *Bock's Car,* the two aircraft that in August 1945 dropped the first atomic bombs over Hiroshima and Nagasaki. The Omaha plant boasted 33 consecutive months of on-schedule production. No other aircraft assembly plant in the United States even came close to the record of the Glenn L. Martin Nebraska Company.

During the Cold War, Offutt Air Force Base – where the former B-26 production plant was located – became the home of the Strategic Air Command (SAC). The former Marauder assembly line was remodeled in 1959 and became a guided missile assembly plant for SAC's new inventory of intercontinental missiles.

A distinctive feature of the B-26 C-45-MO was the application of the Army Air Corps stenciling on the upper armor plate. This French B-26 C-45-MO (Serial Number 42-107564) belonged to the Groupe de Bombardement II/52 "Franche Comté" and was based at Y-6 Lyon-Bron airfield in France during the winter of 1944-1945. This Marauder carries the two squadron insignias of the Groupe de Bombardement II/52 on the lower armor plate. (Musée de l'Air)

The square covering for the drift meter bracket identifies this Marauder as a B-26 C-45-MO. This covering was only applied on the left side of the nose. The Block 45 built by Glenn L. Martin in Omaha, Nebraska, became the sole block to be equipped with a square covering. Baltimore-built B-26 Bs had a shield-shaped cover. Olive drab camouflaged B-26 C-45-MOs were delivered until January 1944. (Jack K. Havener)

B-26 C-45-MO (42-107685) ER-V of the 322nd Bomb Group, 450th Bomb Squadron heads to Normandy on D-Day. The silver aircraft's tail fin was painted olive drab on the Omaha production line. All silver C-45-MOs were first delivered in January 1944. (Harry Holmes)

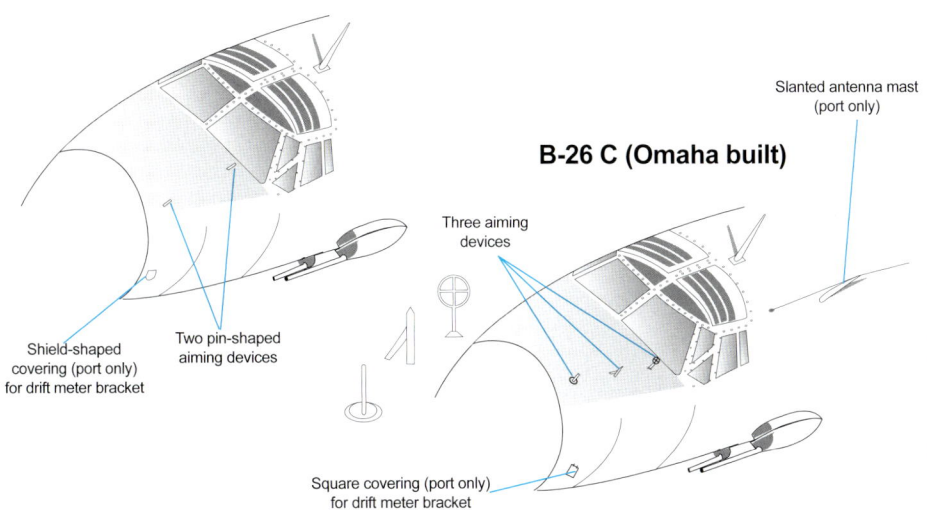

As Marauder units moved to Continental Europe, a number of silver aircraft were painted in olive drab overall, such as this B-26 C-45-MO (42-107697). The Army Air Corps stenciling on the upper armor plate as well the cockpit frame remained in natural silver. *Battlin' Benny* flew as KS-P for the 387th Bomb Group, 557th Bomb Squadron and had accomplished 91 missions by VE-Day. (Alan Crouchman)

Baltimore-Omaha Production Features

B-26 B (Baltimore built)

- Shield-shaped covering (port only) for drift meter bracket
- Two pin-shaped aiming devices

B-26 C (Omaha built)

- Slanted antenna mast (port only)
- Three aiming devices
- Square covering (port only) for drift meter bracket

B-26 C-45-MO Development

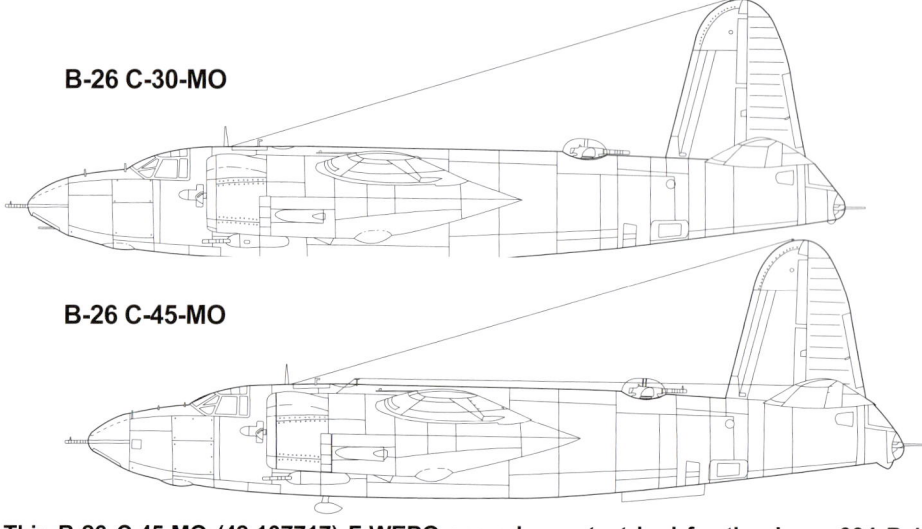

B-26 C-30-MO

B-26 C-45-MO

Flying in a tight formation on their way to a target are four Marauders of the 320th Bomb Group: two B-26 C-45 MOs (Battle Number 80 and 81), the veteran B-26 B-10-MA *Idiot's Delight* (Battle Number 93), and a freshly assigned B-26 G-5-MA (43-34240).

B-26 C-45-MO (42-107831) was one of the last Marauders built at Glenn L. Martin in Omaha, Nebraska. The blue Battle Number 68 indicates it belongs to the Group de Bombardement I/19 "Gascogne." (ECPA)

This B-26 C-45-MO (42-107717) F-WEPO served as a test bed for the Jumo 004 B-1. The German jet engine had been mounted by the French company SNECMA in the rear fuselage of the Marauder, replacing the tail turret position. A large air intake duct had been mounted on both sides on the fuselage of this B-26 C-45-MO during the tests, which were conducted at the Villacoublay air base in the summer of 1948. This Marauder continued to serve as a test bed until June 1951 and was subsequently scrapped. (Michel Cristescu)

The nose art on this B-26 C-45-MO (42-107752) Battle Number 88 was applied by Sgt. Vernon Prince, the most talented unit artist of the 320th Bomb Group. Subsequently the nickname *Miss Arkansas* was added on the nose of this Marauder. *Miss Arkansas* was one of the most attractive Marauders in the entire 42nd Bomb Wing. The upper package machine gun has been deleted. The ground crew under the command of Crew Chief T/Sgt. Harry Bacon poses at Y-9 Dijon-Longvic airbase in France in March 1945. This particular Marauder was given to the French Air Force after World War II. (Victor C. Tannehill)

A formation of B-26 C-45-MOs of the Groupe de Bombardement II/20 "Bretagne" display their unit marking, a blue Croix de Lorraine (Cross of Lorraine). The white rectangle part of the U.S. national emblem has been deleted on a number of Marauders (ECPA)

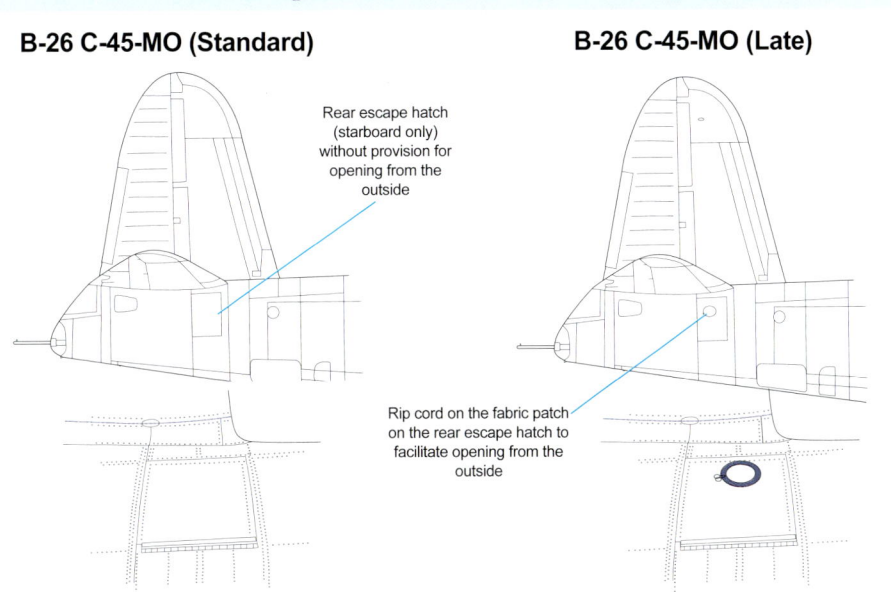

Barracuda was a B-26 C-45-MO (42-107666) belonging as Y5-F to the 344th Bomb Group, 495th Bomb Squadron. The original Army Air Corps stenciling on the upper armor plate had been deleted to make room for the eye of the nose art. The information were hand written below the anti-glare panel. (Arthur M. Brewer via Jack K. Havener)

Rear Escape Hatch Development

B-26 C-45-MO (Standard)

Rear escape hatch (starboard only) without provision for opening from the outside

B-26 C-45-MO (Late)

Rip cord on the fabric patch on the rear escape hatch to facilitate opening from the outside

JM-1 US Navy

A total of 225 JM-1 (Bureau of Aeronautics numbers 66595 through 66794 and 75183 through 75207) served with the U.S. Navy as target tugs. The first JM-1s were delivered in September 1943.

The JM-1 aircraft that saw service were far from being identical. A number were equipped with the small carburetor air intakes of the B-26 A, but the majority had the large carburetor air intakes that became standard on the B-26 B/C. Some JM-1s had the small, rectangular antenna mast of the B-26 A, while others had the tall triangular antenna mast of the B-26 B/C bomber variant. Most JM-1s had the B-26 A type Plexiglas nose without the V-shaped brace that was a feature on most B-26 Bs. However there were in fact some JM-1 in operation with the V-shaped brace in the nose.

Early models of the JM-1 lacked a centerline mounted vent mast on the upper fuselage at the wing root section, while late JM-1 were fitted with this vent mast for the fuselage main tanks.

A large antenna, which was centerline mounted on the lower fuselage, as well a centerline-mounted rail on the lower fuselage surfaces were two dedicated features of the Navy JM-1s.

All JM-1s were equipped with a rectangular entrance door with a window on the starboard rear fuselage, just below the horizontal stabilizer. Another Navy modification was rarely seen on the JM-1: the slight offset of the teardrop shaped covering for the radio compass to the starboard.

This JM-1 (Bureau of Aeronautics number 75189) has a V-shaped brace on the Plexiglas nose, which was not often seen on the JM-1. The target tug has the drop shaped housing for the radio compass slightly offset to starboard, which is non standard. (U.S. Navy)

JM-1 Development

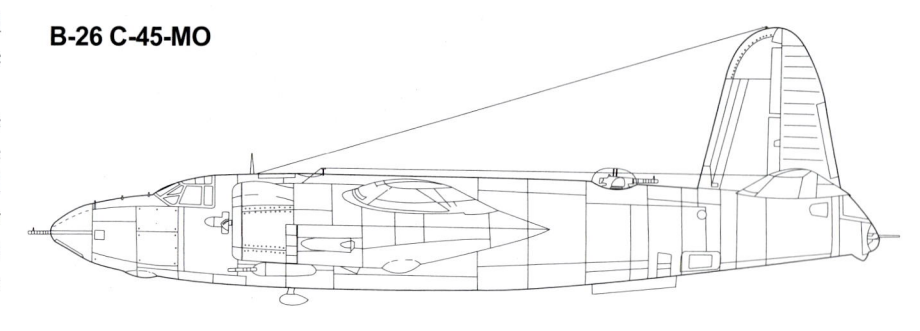

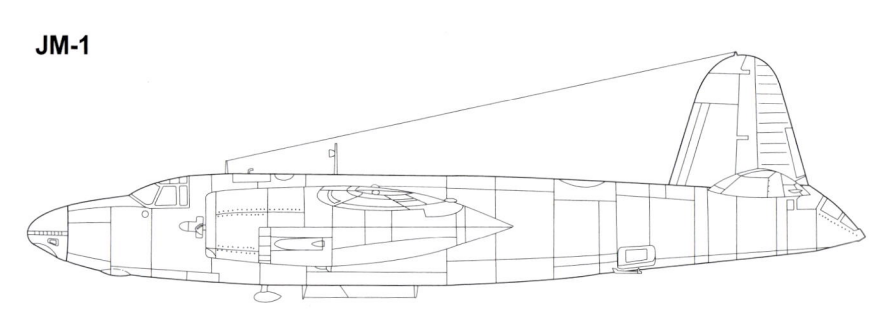

B-26 C-45-MO

JM-1

JM-1 (Bureau number 77622) warms up its engines on 23 December 1943. The standard production JM-1 is equipped with a Plexiglas nose without a V-shaped brace and has a centerline-mounted teardrop-shaped housing for the radio compass. (GLMMAM)

JM-1 Test Bed

The Glenn L. Martin Company in Baltimore converted one JM-1 aircraft (Bureau of Aeronautics number 66599) for use as a test bed for the axial flow Westinghouse 19-B turbo jet. Testing began under U.S. Navy supervision in June 1946.

It was for the Navy that Westinghouse Electric originally launched development of this first practical jet engine of wholly American design in October 1941. With an output of 1,365 lbs of thrust at 18,000 r.p.m., the first example entered the testing phase in March 1943. The Westinghouse 19-B, with a six-stage axial compressor and a single-stage turbine, subsequently became the J30 and was installed in the McDonnell FH-1 Phantom, the first pure jet fighter designed specifically for the U.S. Navy. The J30 also powered the Northrop X-4 Bantam as well the Northrop XP-79 Flying Ram.

The Westinghouse 19-B was installed in the tail end of the JM-1. Two air intake scoops were located on the sides of the rear fuselage and were mounted just forward of the engine. The air flowed from the scoops to the engine through ducts that joined at the air intake. A firewall with a window allowed the performance of the jet engine to be observed. A small inlet was installed on the port side just below the tail gunner's square window. The tail canopy was also redesigned on the JM-1 test bed, with a circular aperture cut in the tail cone to make room for the engine nozzle.

To feed air to the Westinghouse 19-B jet engine in the tail of the converted JM-1 (Bureau Number 66599), two large air scoops were added, one on each side of the rear fuselage. The small inlet aft of the national marking was only on the port side. (GLMMAM)

This converted JM-1 (Bureau of Aeronautics number 66599) served as a test bed for the Westinghouse 19-B axial flow turbo jet. With the exception of the Yellow tail, the test bed remained in natural silver. (GLMMAM)

45

Marauder II (B-26 C-33-MO)

The British Royal Air Force (RAF) operated a total of 123 Marauder II aircraft, all of which were built by the Glenn L. Martin Nebraska Company at Omaha under the contract AC-19342 in the course of 1943. These B-26s received the RAF serials FB400 through FB522. There were 104 Marauder IIs built in the B-26 C-30-MO block. In order to distinguish these aircraft on the production line from the Marauders for the Army Air Corps, these planes received the designation B-26 C-33-MO. The first 19 B-26 C-45-MOs (42-107497 through 42-107515) built were also allocated to the RAF (FB493 through FB511). All these Marauder IIs were delivered under Lend-Lease aid. The Royal Air Force Marauder IIs were delivered in standard Army Air Corps camouflage, but with British national markings and serials.

The British Marauder II differed in a number of details from the Army Air Corps B-26 C-30-MO. The pin-shaped aiming device in front of the pilot's windscreen was relocated. These Marauder IIs received a small slanted antenna mast on top of the port fuselage, close to the wing root section. An antenna cable connected this mast to the leading edge of the port horizontal stabilizer. This slanted antenna subsequently became standard on the B-26 C-45-MO for the Army Air Corps, the last Marauder block to be built in Omaha. In contrast to the Army Air Corps B-26 C-30-MO, the Marauder II lacked the shark-tooth-shaped tab on the rear wing tip. Mounted on the centerline of the lower rear fuselage was a pin shaped antenna that was not present on any Army Air Corps B-26 C-30-MO. This pin shaped antenna was, however, subsequently introduced on the B-26 F-1-MA of the Army Air Corps. All Marauder IIs lacked the vane on top of the Pitot tube on the both sides of the outer wing leading edges. However, this was not a dedicated RAF feature; a number of USAAF B-26 Cs lacked this vane as well. A number of Marauder IIs were delivered without the two armor plates on the port cockpit section, but the majority of the planes were fitted with these protective shields against Flak and enemy fighters. According RAF specifications, there were also a number of internal changes made in the equipment. Mounted in all Marauder IIs was the British-built Mark XIV bomb sight, and all those aircraft also featured shackles designed to take British bombs.

The RAF handed over its main delivery of the Marauder IIs to the South African Air Force, which allocated the aircraft to Squadrons No. 12 and No. 24. The latter unit started bombing enemy targets on Crete and the Aegean islands in January 1944. Both squadrons were based in March 1944 at Campo Marino.

This Marauder II had been sent to Britain for evaluation by various Royal Air Force institutions. Built under contract AC-19342 with the Army Air Corps serial number 41-35438 as a B-26 C-33-MO, this Marauder eventually became FB436 in RAF service. (Royal Air Force Museum)

Nose art was popular among the Marauder units of the South African Air Force. This Marauder II had been nicknamed *Honky Tonk* by its crew and carry the individual aircraft letter "X." The aircraft had left the Glenn L. Martin Nebraska Company at Omaha as a B-26 C-33-MO. The mission markings were applied above the individual letter. (Department of Defense)

Marauder II Development

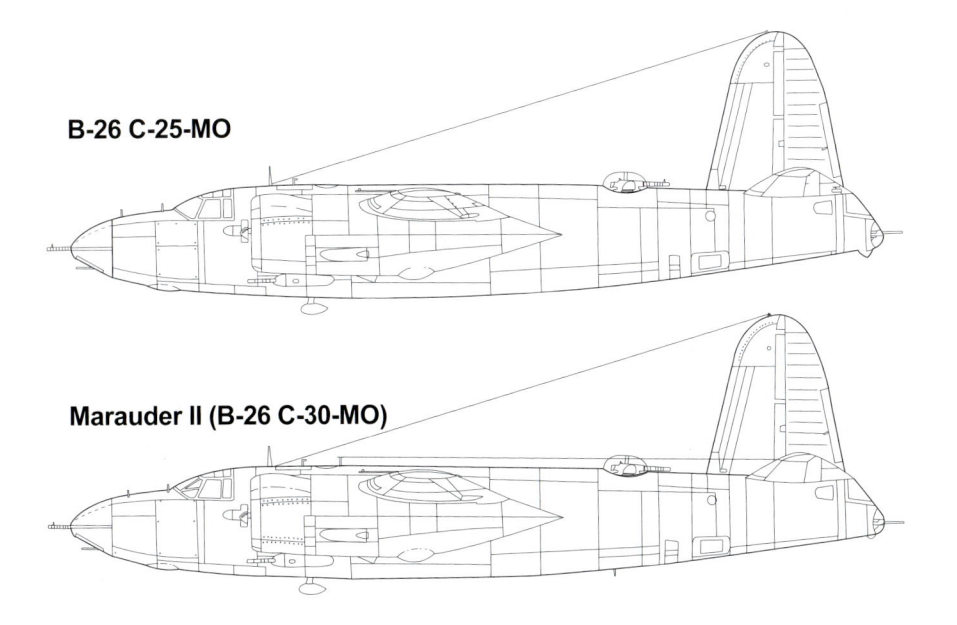

B-26 C-25-MO

Marauder II (B-26 C-30-MO)

The No. 12 Squadron of the South African Air Force had attacked a bridge over the Esino river near Chiaravalle in the Province of Ancona. Marauder II FB 442 is leaving the target close to the Adriatic coast of Italy. This aircraft was built as a B-26 C-33-MO (41-35444) and received at No. 12 Squadron the individual aircraft letter "D." This Marauder II was struck of charge on 31 May 1945. (Department of Defense)

B-26 F-1-MA

The Marauder wing on the B-26 F-1-MA was significantly redesigned, with the intention of shortening the take-off and landing runs. This modification was done in a way that the angle of incidence was increased by 3½ degrees, giving the engines a slight upwards tilt. This modification shortened the take-off run of a combat-loaded B-26 by some 100 yards and reduced the take-off speed to about 110 miles per hour. The landing run was shortened by a quarter. During flight, the wing modification gave the B-26 F-1-MA a slight tail-up attitude increasing drag and slightly reducing the Marauder's top speed to 277 miles per hour.

The B-26 F-1-MA became the first Marauder variant to be equipped with a centerline mounted vent mast, which was located on top of the fuselage close to the wing root section. This mast ventilated the B-26 F-1-MA's two main wing tanks, each of which had a fuel capacity of 360 U.S. gallons (1,362 liters). The fuel system of the B-26 F-1-MA had no cross feed, which meant that each R-2800-43 engine was supplied by a separate system, consisting of the 360-U.S. gallon (1,362-liter) main fuel tanks and the outer 121-U.S. gallon (458-liter) auxiliary tank.

A enlarged oval windshield in the lower Plexiglas section was introduced on the B-26 F-1-MA. This enlarged windshield touched the horizontal frame of the Plexiglas nose. The previous B-26 B/C variants all had a smaller oval windshield. The aperture for the fixed machine gun in the starboard lower Plexiglas nose was deleted from the B-26 F-1-MA. This aperture in the Plexiglas nose was mounted on the B and C models. The aperture was, however, faired over with an oval piece of Plexiglas when the fixed machine gun was not mounted.

The B-26 F-1-MA adopted the three aiming device configuration in front of the left cockpit windshield from the B-26 C-45-MO, however the support strut on the middle pin-shaped sight was deleted on the B-26 F-1-MA.

The B-26 F-1-MA took over the small slanted antenna on the port fuselage from the B-26 C-45-MO. An antenna cable fixed on the port wing leading edge of the horizontal tailplane connected this mast.

A direct take over from the Royal Air Force Marauder II was the small pin-shaped antenna that was mounted on the centerline of the rear lower fuselage. This antenna had never been carried by any of the previous B-26 B/C models.

The starboard rear escape hatch for the tail gunner was modified in a way that the hatch could be also opened from the outside. With the exception of late production B-26 C-45-MO models, all B-26 B/Cs lacked this feature. These B-26 F-1-MAs had a circular aperture that was covered with a fabric patch and fitted with a rip cord. Removing the fabric patch by pulling the rip cord gave access to the latch, allowing the tail gunner's hatch to be opened.

All B-26 F-1-MAs were delivered from the Middle River plant without the shark-tooth-shaped tab on the wing tip, but a number of aircraft received this tab as a field modification.

One of the first B-26 F-1-MA aircraft has just left the assembly line of the Glenn L. Martin factory at Middle River in Baltimore on 1 February 1944 and has no propellers or markings. The B-26 F-1-MA became the first Marauder variant to be equipped with a centerline-mounted vent mast located on top of the fuselage. With the exception of the nose armament, all Browning M-2 0.50-caliber machine guns were installed. (GLMMAM)

B-26 F-1-MA Development

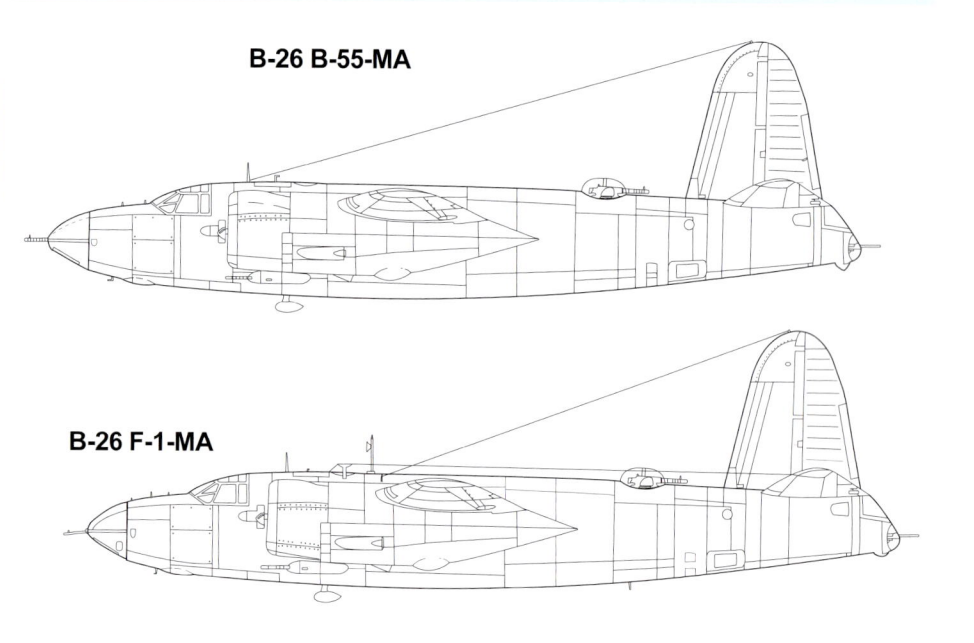

B-26 B-55-MA

B-26 F-1-MA

All B-26 F-1-MAs were delivered with the solid nose wheel of the B-26 B/C model. However, a number of B-26 F-1-MAs were retrofitted as a field modification with the spoked nose wheel without a circular cover plate on the rim. This spoked nose wheel became standard on the subsequent G model.

Minor internal changes of the B-26 F-1-MA incorporated included the rearrangement of some cockpit instruments and an all-electric bomb release. Well liked by the pilots was a mechanical emergency system for lowering the landing gear. This system reduced the need for a belly landing when the vulnerable hydraulics for the undercarriage failed. The wing modification also included an additional fuel capacity of 20 gallons. But these extra gallons made little practical difference to combat range, because of the increased drag generated by the new wing design. The B-26 F-1-MA had a provision for two releasable 250-gallon (946-liter) auxiliary fuel tanks to be mounted in the rear bomb bay. These bomb bay tanks are connected through a breakable union and may be salvoed with the same controls that are used for bomb salvo.

The first of a total of 100 B-26 F-1-MA aircraft (42-96229 through 42-96328) left the assembly line at Baltimore during late February 1944. All these aircraft were delivered in natural silver overall. The first examples of the new type reached the 9th Air Force in the United Kingdom during May 1944. After having received specific 9th Air Force equipment, the B-26 F-1-MAs became operational over occupied Europe in late June 1944. Most deliveries of the B-26 F-1-MA were made to the 9th Air Force in Britain, while only a few examples were allocated to the 12th Air Force in the Mediterranean Theater of Operation.

B-26 F-1-MA (42-96268) crashed on a formation practice flight with 2nd Lt. Verne Thompson at the controls at A-71 Clastres airbase in France on 28 November 1944. The unit code FW-H identifies the Marauder as belonging to the 387th Bomb Group, 556th Bomb Squadron. Before this crash, this B-26 F-1-MA had flown 22 missions with the 387th Bomb Group, the first on 6 September 1944. (Bob Allen via Alan Crouchman)

The U.S. Navy evaluated this factory fresh B-26 F-1-MA (42-96239) at Patuxent River, Maryland, in early March 1944. It was one of the first examples of the F-variant to be built by Martin's Middle River plant. This Marauder crashed on 18 September 1944 at Scott Field airbase near Belleville, Illinois. (GLMMAM)

Nose Development

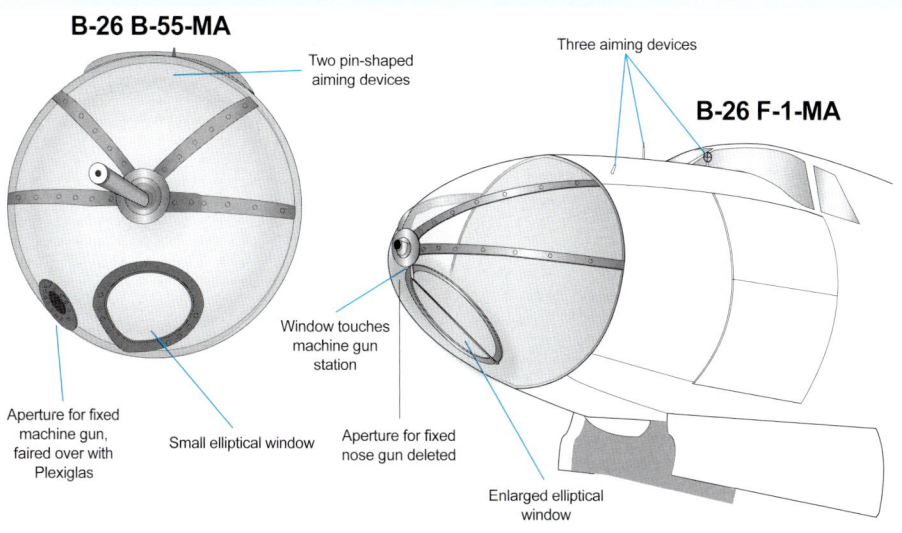

B-26 B-55-MA
- Two pin-shaped aiming devices
- Aperture for fixed machine gun, faired over with Plexiglas
- Small elliptical window

B-26 F-1-MA
- Three aiming devices
- Window touches machine gun station
- Aperture for fixed nose gun deleted
- Enlarged elliptical window

49

This B-26 F-1-MA (42-96276) flew with the unit marking KS-N for the 387th Bomb Group, 557th Bomb Squadron. *Miss Behavin'* had left Martin's factory at Middle River in natural silver, but was subsequently camouflaged on olive drab overall. *Miss Behavin'* flew her first mission on 19 July 1944 and survived the war with 69 missions on her credit. (Bob Allen via Alan Crouchman)

Nose Wheel Development

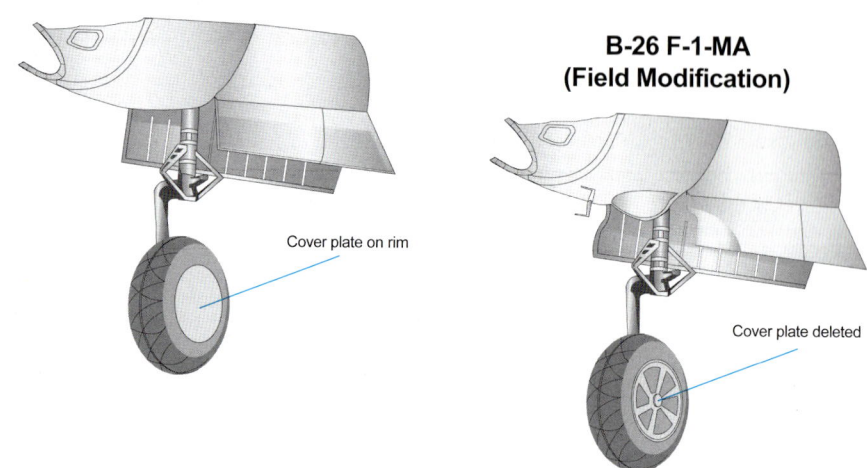

B-26 F-1-MA (Factory Fitted)

Cover plate on rim

B-26 F-1-MA (Field Modification)

Cover plate deleted

This B-26 F-1-MA (42-96281) *Redlight Rosie* with the unit marking 5W-V was assigned to the 394th Bomb Group, 587th Bomb Squadron. Sporting a spiral painted on her spinners, *Redlight Rosie* operated from A-74 Cambrais-Niergnies in France, and flew a total of 107 missions. The enlarged oval windshield of the B-26 F-1-MA is a typical feature of this variant. Earlier Marauder variants had smaller windshields. (Alain Pelletier)

This B-26 F-1-MA (42-96256) *Ugly Duckling* with the unit marking RJ-J is an early model assigned to the 323rd Bomb Group, 454th Bomb Squadron. The shark tooth tab on the rear wing tip is a field modification; no B-26 F-1-MA was ever fitted with such tabs on the production line. *Ugly Duckling* received her overall olive drab camouflage paint job at the group level. She was badly shot up during a mission to the marshalling yard at Memmingen on 20 April 1945. (Robert M. Radlein via Robert Forsyth)

Marauder III

After turning out 100 B-26 F-1-MAs for the Army Air Corps, Martin's Middle River plant built another 200 of the F models for the Royal Air Force (HD402 through HD601). These aircraft received the British designation Marauder III. The Army Air Corps designation for the first 100 Marauders (42-96329 through 42-96428) had been B-26 F-2-MA. The second batch (42-96429 through 42-96528) received the designation B-26 F-6-MA.

The first Marauder IIIs were completed in March 1944 and delivered to Italian based units of the South African Air Force (SAAF) during mid-summer 1944. The steadily flow of this type enabled the SAAF to create two new units, the Nos. 21 and 30 Squadrons. Together with the veteran units, Nos. 12 and 24 Squadrons, they were incorporated into the No. 3 Wing, based at Pescara, Italy. The No. 3 Wing had an active strength of 70 aircraft and its main task was to support Allied ground operations on the Eastern side of Italy. In addition, missions against targets in Austria and Yugoslavia were also flown.

In contrast to the Army Air Corps practice, the Royal Air Force continued to camouflage the Marauder III in dark olive drab on the upper surfaces and natural gray on the under surfaces.

The Marauder III (B-26 F-2-MA) differed from the American B-26 F-1-MA in having exchanged the Bell M-6 tail turret for a Bell M-6 A tail turret. On the Bell M-6 A, a canvas cover replaced the bulbous Plexiglas tail cap. With the introduction of the Bell M-6 A, the tail was slightly redesigned: the rounded end skin on the M-6 turret with its clear tail cap was replaced by straight-line skinning on the tail.

During the course of production of the B-26 F-2-MA at Middle River, the solid nose wheel was replaced by a spoked nose wheel. The B-26 F-6-MA differed from the B-26 F-2MA in that the centerline-mounted vent-mast was replaced by a periscope-shaped mast located further aft and to the starboard. In contrast to the vent mast of the B-26 F-2-MA that vented only the two main wing tanks, the vent-boom vented both the main and auxiliary fuel tanks in the wing. The B-26 F-6-MA was equipped from the beginning of production with the spoked nose wheel. Both the spoked wheel and the vent-boom were subsequently adopted by the B-26 G-1-MA of the U.S. Army Air Corps.

The Royal Air Force and South African Air Force received as additional Lend-Lease aid 75 B-26 G-11-MAs (43-34465 through 43-34539), which were given the British serial numbers HD602 through HD676. They also received 75 B-26 G-21-MAs (44-67990 through 44-68064), for which the RAF issued the registration numbers HD677 through HD751.

Neither the Royal Air Force nor the South African Air Force distinguished between the B-26 F-2 and F-6 and B-26 G; both variants were simply known as Marauder III.

This Marauder III belonging to the South African Air Force carries the insignia of the No. 3 Wing, which had its headquarters at Pescara, Italy. This B-26 F-6-MA is non standard, since it features a square covering for the drift meter bracket on the right nose. This cover appears to be a dedicated South African field modification. Overall silver Marauder IIIs were extremely rare in SAAF service. (Department of Defense)

The No. 109 Repair and Salvage Unit of the South African Air Force at Bari in Southern Italy dismantles the Marauder III HD521, that once left Martin's Middle River plant at Baltimore as a B-26 F-6-MA (42-96448). The Marauder III flew with the individual aircraft letter "F" for the No. 12 Squadron. The B-26 F-6-MA overshot the runway at Rimini air base at the Adriatic coast on 8 February 1945. (Department of Defense)

This Marauder III HD620 had been allocated to the No. 12 Squadron and carried the individual aircraft letter "R" on the nose and the rear fuselage. This plane was built as a B-26 G-11-MA (43-34558) at Martin's Middle River plant at Baltimore under Lend-Lease aid for the British Commonwealth. This Marauder III crashed during a mission on 29 December 1944, after being severely damaged by the explosion of Marauder III HD501. (Department of Defense)

This is one of the last B-26 F-6-MA (Marauder III) built for the Royal Air Force under Lend-Lease aid. This aircraft is parked at the ramp of Martin's Middle River plant beside the third built B-26 G-1-MA (43-34117). All B-26 F-6-MA aircraft had spoked wheels and periscope-shaped vent-boom on the upper rear fuselage. In contrast to the contemporary B-26s for the Army Air Corps, all Royal Air Force Marauder III were delivered camouflaged. (GLMMAM)

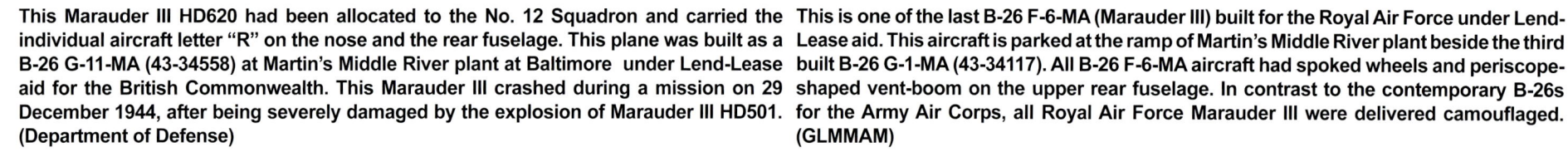

Tail Turret Development

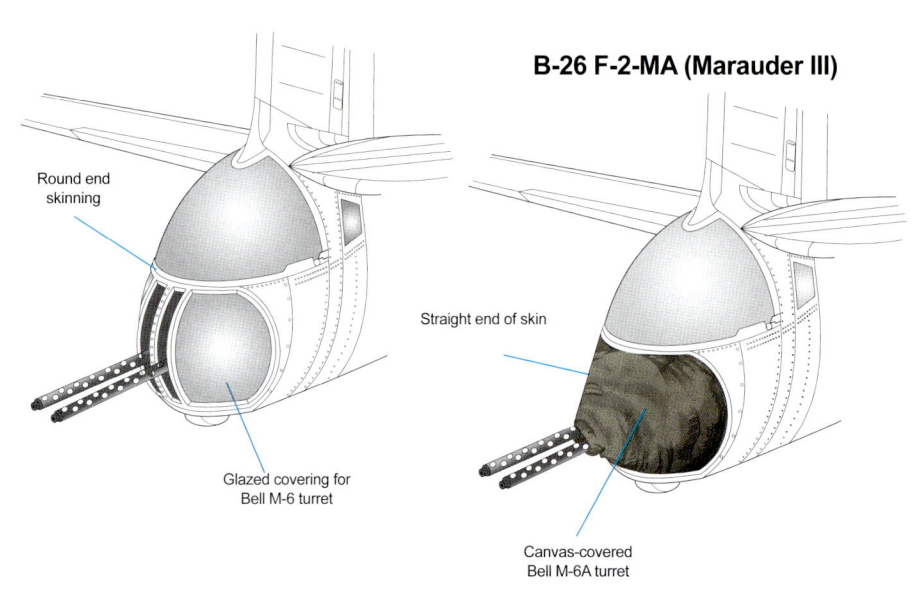

B-26 F-1-MA

B-26 F-2-MA (Marauder III)

- Round end skinning
- Glazed covering for Bell M-6 turret
- Straight end of skin
- Canvas-covered Bell M-6A turret

Bliksem – Africaans for "Lightning" – accomplished between 15 August 1944 and 21 April 1945 a total 108 missions, more than any other Marauder in South African Air Force service. Once built as a B-26 F-6-MA (42-96488), the Marauder III HD561 had been allocated with the individual aircraft letter "B" to the No. 21 Squadron. The veteran was struck off charge on 21 March 1946. (Department of Defense)

B-26 G-1-MA

The B-26 G-1-MA – following the Marauder III (B-26 F-6-MA) on the production line at the Martin Middle River plant – replaced some specific Army Air Corps equipment with more universal Army Navy (AN) equipment, allowing a certain standardization. One piece of this AN equipment was an enlarged life raft that required a larger life raft compartment on the upper fuselage decking, and as a result an enlarged access panel as well. The rectangular access panel of the previous B-26 F-1-MA variant was offset to port. In the B-26 G-1-MA, this panel was square shaped and centerline-mounted. The handle was repositioned and two circular windows were introduced in the access panel for the life raft.

The first B-26 G-1-MAs that left the production line at Middle River were still equipped with the L-shaped Pitot tube of the B-26 F. However, the L-shaped Pitot tube was deleted from the lower nose on the majority of B-26 G-1-MAs and instead a boom shaped Pitot tube was mounted on the port outer wing leading edge. In sharp contrast to the previous B-26 B/C models, no Pitot tube was ever mounted on starboard.

The B-26 G-1-MA became the first block produced at the Middle River plant at Baltimore that received the shark-tooth-shaped tab on the rear wing tip of the production line. Previous B- and F- models had this tab mounted as a field modification only. However, the first few B-26 G-1-MAs produced were delivered without the shark-tooth-shaped tab.

The pin shaped antenna of the B-26 F-1-MA was deleted from the lower rear fuselage of all B-26 G-1-MAs. Instead, a large antenna – identical to that on the B-26 C-45-MO – was mounted centerline on the rear lower fuselage. The B-26 G-1-MA had adopted the Bell M-6 A turret from the Marauder III for the Royal Air Force, becoming the first Army Air Corps B-26 variant to be equipped with this kind of turret. The Bell M-6 A turret replaced the Plexiglas tail cap of the M-6 with a canvas covering.

On the B-26 G-1-MA, both the main and the outer auxiliary wing tanks were vented. As a result, the vent boom had been increased in diameter as well as height and became periscope shaped. This boom was offset to the rear and to starboard, while the smaller vent mast on the B-26 F-1-MA was centerline-mounted. In contrast to the B-26 F-1-MA, the B-26 G-1-MA was equipped with a cross-feed fuel system. Each engine or both engines were supplied from either or both wing tanks through booster pumps.

At the request of the 9th Air Force, the B-26 G-1-MA had been equipped with a C-1 automatic pilot.

The B-26 G-1-MA became the first variant to be painted with large black stripes on the upper wing surface, indicating the no-step area atop the wing.

In all, 100 of the B-26 G-1-MAs (43-34115 through 43-34214) were built under contract AC-31733. The first examples of this type reached the 9th Air Force, operating from bases in the United Kingdom during mid-August 1944.

Most of the B-26 G-1-MAs built by Martin's Middle River plant at Baltimore were delivered to the 9th Air Force, while a small number of this block saw action with the 12th Air Force in the Mediterranean Theater of Operations.

This B-26 G-1-MA (43-34151) became tail-heavy due to a loading error. This Marauder received a field applied camouflage of olive drab overall. For better identification, the area around the squadron marking and the serial number remained in natural silver. This Marauder was one of the very first G-models to be allocated to the 387th Bomb Group. It flew its first mission on 15 August 1944. The ship accomplished a total of 22 missions before KS-A flew into high ground on 25 November 1944. (Lee Sunderlin via Alan Crouchman)

B-26 G-1-MA Development

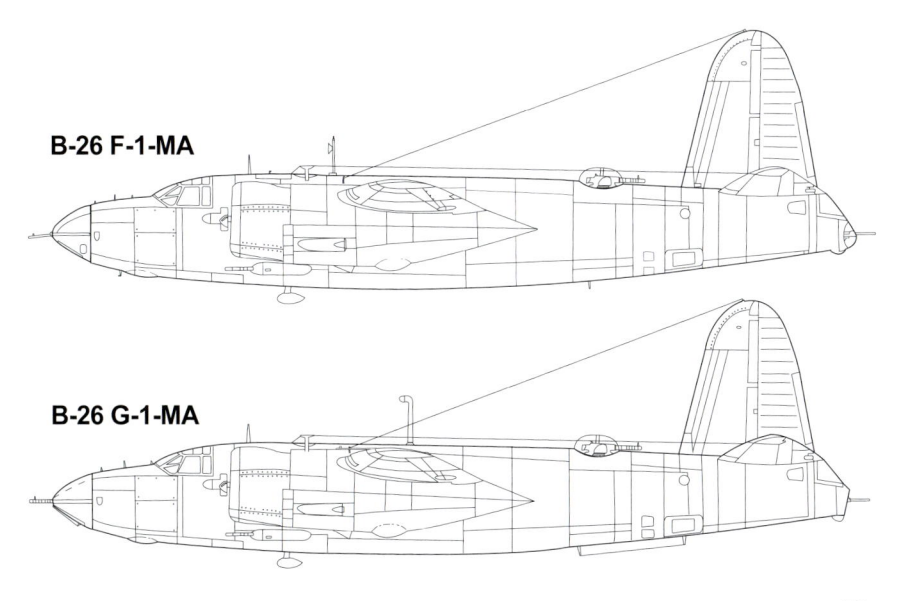

B-26 F-1-MA

B-26 G-1-MA

This B-26 G-1-MA (43-34181) Y5-O *Lak-a-Nookie* had the upper surfaces camouflaged in olive drab, a field modification often seen on the G-model of the Marauder. The small tail shell-case collector applied on the lower tail was a field modification of the 344th Bomb Group. The B-26 G-1-MA had the new Bell M-6 A turret with a canvas covering instead of the Plexiglas covering of the B-26 F-1-MA. (Arthur M. Brewer via Jack K. Havener)

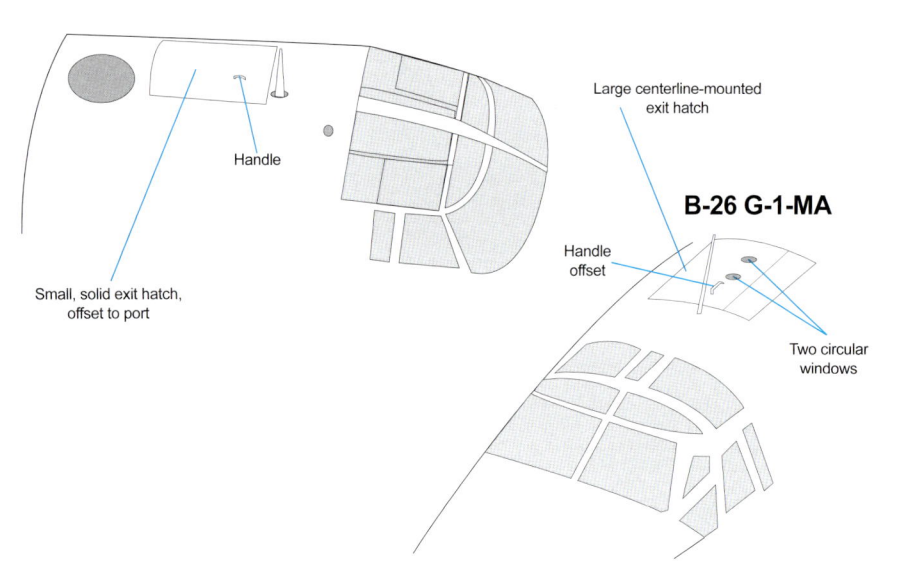

Lak-a-Nookie had accomplished 88 successful missions and even survived a jet fighter attack of Me 262 A-1as belonging to the Jagdverband 44 (Fighter Unit 44) on 25 April 1945. Then a blown tire during a practice flight damaged the Marauder during landing at A-78 Florennes-Juzaine airfield in Belgium on 12 May 1945 beyond economical repair. *Lak-a-Nookie* flew most of its missions with James L. Stalter, the regular pilot. (James L. Stalter via Robert Forsyth)

The field applied olive drab camouflage painted on the upper surfaces became most common on B-26 G-1-MAs when the 9th Air Force moved bases in continental Europe. This B-26 G-1-MA (Serial Number 43-34213) became the 99th and second-last Marauder built in this block. *The Old Goat* belonged with the unit marking 4T-C to the 394th Bomb Group, 585th Bomb Squadron. Unlike most B-26 B/C models, the G-variant generally lacked the vane applied on top of the Pitot tube. (Jerry Scutts via Eddie J. Creek)

Life Raft Panel Development

B-26 F-1-MA

- Handle
- Small, solid exit hatch, offset to port

B-26 G-1-MA

- Large centerline-mounted exit hatch
- Handle offset
- Two circular windows

54

B-26 G-5-MA

The B-26 G-5-MA followed the B-26 G-1-MA on the Martin production line at Middle River. This block was externally identical to the B-26 G-1-MA though it incorporated some minor hydraulic system changes. There were a total of 200 B-26 G-5-MA aircraft (43-34215 through 43-34414) built.

B-26 G-5-MA became the last variant of the Marauder that had a vane mounted on top of the Pitot tube on the port wing leading edge. A substantial number of this block were, however, delivered without the vane on top of the Pitot tube, and all further models of the G-variant lacked this vane.

The majority of all B-26 G-5-MAs were delivered to 9th and 12th Air Force units. The sickle-shaped antenna on top of the cockpit, close to the radio antenna mast, was only mounted by the production line on 12th Air Force Marauders and those delivered to the Free French. The first B-26 G-5-MA became operational with the 9th Air Force during October 1944. The Middle River plant delivered the B-26 G-5-MA in either natural silver overall or with a coat of olive drab applied on the upper surfaces.

The B-26 G-5-MA became the first G-variant to be handled over to the Free French Air Force. Most of the substantial number of B-26 G-5-MAs delivered to the French from Martin's Middle River plant arrived in natural silver.

Many of the French pilots who flew the B-26 G-5-MA were less than satisfied with the new type of Marauder and considered the G-variant to be slower and less stable in the air than the B-26 C-45-MO model which had also been introduced. Like the Marauders belonging to the 12th Air Force, all French B-26 G-5-MA aircraft were equipped with the sickle-shaped antenna, which was mounted close to the radio mast above the cockpit section.

This B-26 G-5-MA (43-34269) – also shown after its rollout at Martin's Middle River Plant near Baltimore in the photo below – had the first three digits of the serial number overpainted on the fabric rudder. This particular Marauder belonged to the Groupe de Bombardement I/32 "Bourgogne" with the Battle number "63." This unit had the Battle Number painted in Green. On the nose of this particular Marauder is the name *Pouilly Fuisse*, is a region belonging to the Bourgogne (Burgundy). (Musée de l'Air)

It is early August 1944 and brand new B-26 G-5-MAs are waiting at the Glenn L. Martin factory field at Middle River to be accepted by the U.S. Army Air Corps. The camouflaged Marauders in the foreground were delivered to the 9th Air Force, while the main part of the natural silver overall B-26 G-5-MAs were transferred to the Free French, including ship 43-34269 – parked in the middle of the two camouflaged Marauders. This B-26 G-5-MA subsequently became *Green 63* in service with the Groupe de Bombardement I/32 "Bourgogne," and is pictured in the photo above of this page. (GLMMAM)

Tail shell-case collector (9th, 12th AF)

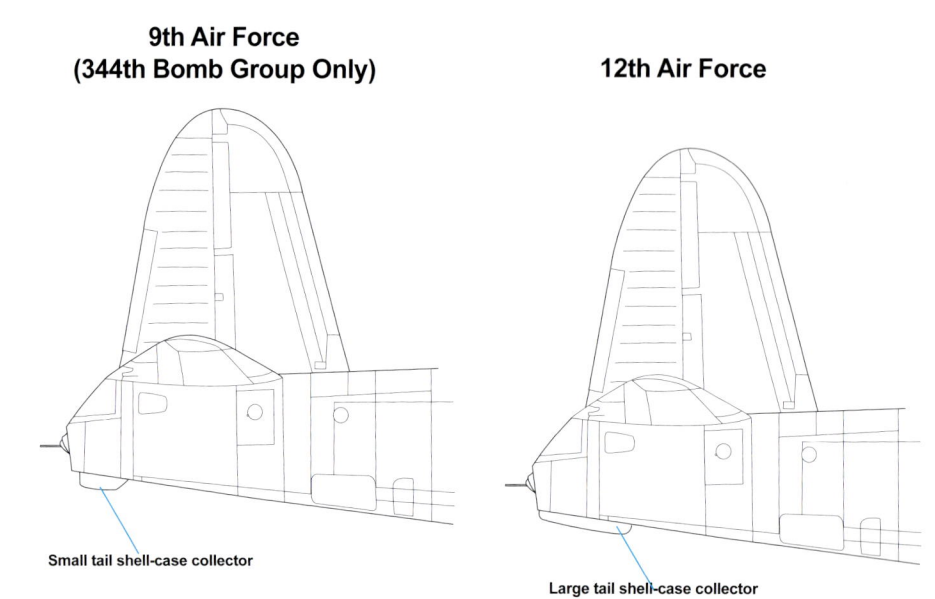

9th Air Force (344th Bomb Group Only)

12th Air Force

Small tail shell-case collector

Large tail shell-case collector

This B-26 G-5-MA (43-34413) warms up its Pratt & Whitney R-2800-43 Double Wasp at A-60 Beaumont-sur-Oise air base in France. The Marauder belonged with the unit marking RU-D to the 386th Bomb Group, 554th Bomb Squadron and carried the nickname *Margie*. This particular Marauder was subsequently transferred to the 394th Bomb Group and received the new group marking 5W-F. (Harry Holmes)

During the harsh winter of 1944-1945, ground crewmen clear snow off of a B-26 G-5-MA (43-34348) at A-69 Laon-Athies in France. This Marauder with the unit marking RJ-A belonged to the 323rd Bomb Group, 454th Bomb Squadron. This B-26 G-5-MA was declared as salvage on 9 February 1945. (Steve Birdsall)

A brand new B-26 G-5-MA belonging to the Free French Air Force is being maintained. Most of the B-26 Cs and B-26 Gs allocated to the French allies were new aircraft. This Marauder still carry the original gun package, but most French units had deleted on or two machine guns on each side. (ECPA)

B-26 G-10-MA

The B-26 G-10-MA became the first Marauder variant with a tail shell-case collector mounted on Martin's production line at Middle River. All previous models that had been equipped with the tail shell-case collector had this item mounted as a retrofit. The tail shell-case collector was only introduced on Marauders assigned to the 12th Air Force, Mediterranean Theater of Operation. With the exception of some few B-26s from the 344th Bomb Group, none of the 9th Air Force Marauders were retrofitted with a tail shell-case collector.

The tail shell-case collector was introduced because a 0.50-caliber casing spent by the Bell M-6 A tail turret could easily smash through the Plexiglas of aircraft flying lower in the formation and cause serious damage. Unlike with the tail shell-casing collectors that were retrofitted on 12th Air Force Marauders and were rectangular with rounded ends, those mounted at the factory on the lower tail of the B-26 G-10-MA, were all wedge shaped. Like the B-26 G-5-MAs, the B-26 G-10-MAs left the factory either in natural silver or camouflaged on the upper surfaces.

A total of 125 B-26 G-10-MA aircraft were produced for the Army Air Corps in two blocks (43-34415 through 43-34464 and 43-34540 through 43-34614). Between these two blocks, an order for 75 B-26 G-11-MAs had been built for the Royal Air Force.

The Marauder nearest the camera was nicknamed *El Lobo* ("The Wolf") and had a wolf head painted on the starboard nose. This B-26 G-10-MA (43-34566), assigned to the 397th Bomb Group, 597th Bomb Squadron, only carries the squadron marking (9F) but no individual aircraft letter on the tail. (Paul Gardella via Jack K. Havener)

Free French Marauder belonging to the Groupe de Bombardement I/32 "Bourgogne" fly in formation. The Battle Number Green 61 of the B-26 G-10-MA (43-34591) is painted over the Army Air Corps serial number, which was very common on Free French B-26s. (Musée de l'Air)

Tail shell-case collector (B-26 G)

B-26 G-5-MA — No tail shell-case collector

B-26 G-10-MA — Tail shell-case collector

57

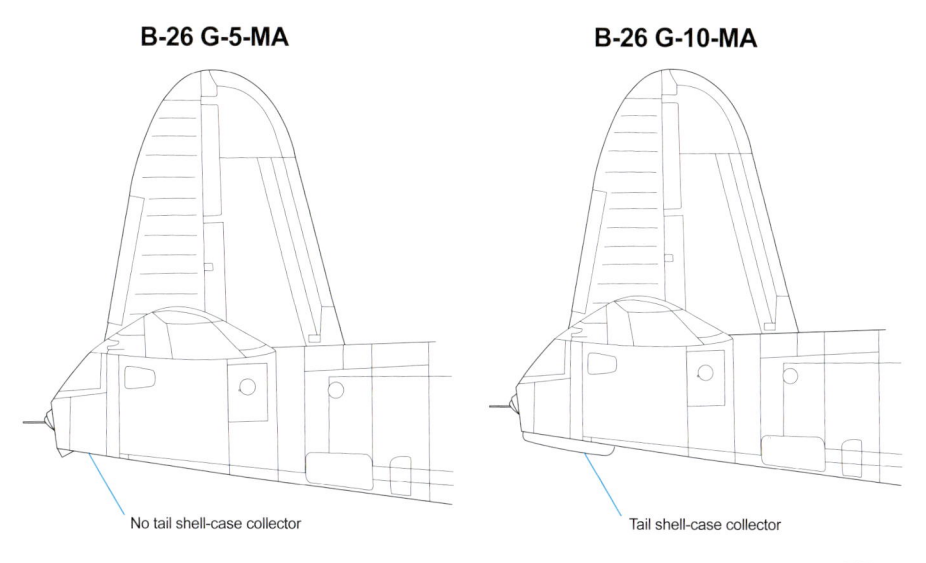

B-26 G-15-MA

The Glenn L. Martin Company turned out a total of 140 B-26 G-15-MA aircraft (44-67805 through 44-67944) under Army Air Corps Contract AC-1871 at the Middle River plant in Baltimore, Maryland.

The B-26 G-15-MA differed from the B-26 G-10-MA in having the sickle shaped antenna mounted atop the cockpit on port beside the antenna mast on all aircraft. On previous G-versions, this sickle shaped antenna was only fitted by Martin's production line at Middle River in Baltimore on Marauders being allocated to the 12th Air Force and the Free French Air Force. The bulk of the Marauders manufactured in the G-15 Block were assigned to the Bomb Group belonging to the 9th Air Force.

The C-1 automatic pilot was deleted from the B-26 G-15-MA. This short-lived device had been introduced on the B-26 G-1-MA.

B-26 G-15-MAs were delivered either in overall silver or with the upper surfaces camouflaged in olive drab. The B-26 G-15-MA was the first block on which Martin's Middle River plant applied the national marking further forward on the rear fuselage. Previous blocks had worn the national marking aft of the circular observation window.

The TB-26 G-15-MA was the trainer version of the B-26 G-15-MA with all defense armament and armor protection deleted. These advanced trainers received a conical tail with a fixed tail canopy. The circular aperture in the upper rear fuselage caused by the missing Martin 250 CE turret was faired over. Ten TB-26 G-15-MAs were built (44-67945 through 44-67954). A number of these aircraft were transferred as JM-2s to the U.S. Navy in March 1945.

B-26 G-20-MA

The B-26 G-20-MA was technically identical to the B-26 G-15-MA. In contrast to the preceding blocks of the B-26 G, all aircraft belonging to the B-26 G-20-MA block were camouflaged on the upper surfaces at the production line, while the lower surfaces remained in natural silver. A total of 60 B-26 G-20-MAs were built for the Army Air Corps in two blocks (44-67970 through 44-67989 and 44-68065 through 44-68104).

Fifteen advanced trainers were built under the designation TB-26 G-20-MA (44-67955 through 44-67969). These aircraft were identical to the previous block of TB-26 G-15-MAs. A number of these advanced trainers were later transferred to the U.S. Navy under the designation JM-2.

B-26 G-21-MA

The B-26 G-21-MA became a variant specifically built for the needs of the Royal Air Force under Army Air Corps contract AC-1871. Seventy-five B-26 G-21-MAs (44-67990 through 44-68064) were built between two blocks of B-26 G-20-MAs made for the Army Air Corps. The Royal Air Force serials HD677 through HD751 were allocated to these B-26 G-21-MAs, which were all designated "Marauder III" in British service.

Serial Number 44-67805 became the first Marauder of the B-26 G-15-MA block. This particular aircraft rolled out in late August 1944. Like most Marauder of Block 15, all these aircraft on the ramp at Middle River were camouflage in olive drab on the upper surfaces. The fairing on the lower tail is the tail shell-case collector. The B-26 G-15-MA became the first block having the national marking applied further forward on the rear fuselage. Previous blocks had the national marking applied behind the circular observation window. This B-26 G-15-MA departed the United States on 8 October 1944 and subsequently joined the 344th Bomb Group, 9th Air Force. The aircraft is listed as salvaged on 7 February 1945 due to battle damage. (GLMMAM)

This B-26 G-15-MA (Serial Number 44-67844) flew as TQ-T for the 387th Bomb Group, 559th Bomb Squadron. The Marauder made its debut with the group on New Year's Day 1945 and accomplished 46 missions until the VE-Day. This particular Marauder had been delivered in natural silver overall, while the majority of this block was camouflaged on the upper surfaces. The Marauder is undergoing maintenance in early 1945 at its hardstand at A-71 Clastres airbase in France. (via Alan Crouchman)

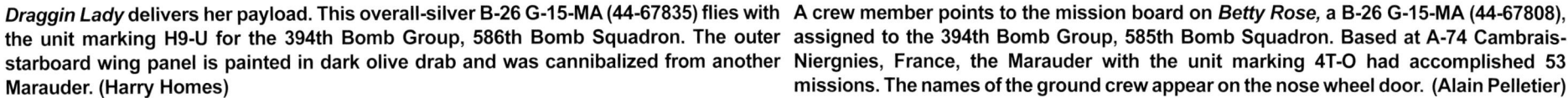

Draggin Lady delivers her payload. This overall-silver B-26 G-15-MA (44-67835) flies with the unit marking H9-U for the 394th Bomb Group, 586th Bomb Squadron. The outer starboard wing panel is painted in dark olive drab and was cannibalized from another Marauder. (Harry Homes)

On 2 January 1945, ground crewmen clean snow off of a grounded Marauder at A-64 St. Dizier airbase in France, where the 387th Bomb Group had to divert due to bad weather. The B-26 G-15-MA (44-67889) had been allocated with the unit marking KX-B to the 387th Bomb Group, 558th Bomb Squadron. Being nicknamed *Command Performance* by its crew, the Marauder accomplished its first mission just on this 2 January 1945. (Alan Crouchman Collection)

A crew member points to the mission board on *Betty Rose*, a B-26 G-15-MA (44-67808), assigned to the 394th Bomb Group, 585th Bomb Squadron. Based at A-74 Cambrais-Niergnies, France, the Marauder with the unit marking 4T-O had accomplished 53 missions. The names of the ground crew appear on the nose wheel door. (Alain Pelletier)

This B-26 G-15-MA (44-67942) belonging to the Groupe de Bombardement I/19 "Gascogne" was the third-last aircraft built in this block by the Glenn L. Martin Company in Baltimore. Marauders from this block assigned to the 12th Air Force and the Free French Air Force in the Mediterranean Theater of Operation left the Middle River plant in natural silver. All Free French Air Force Marauders carried a French fin flash. The eight-foot battle number 66 as well the tail band are applied in blue. (Michel Cristescu)

B-26 G-25-MA

The B-26 G-25-MA became the final variant of the Marauder. There were a total of 118 examples built (Serial Number 44-68105 through 44-68221, plus 44-68254). The B-26 G-25-MA differed in a number of small modifications from the previous blocks of the G-model. Deleted from all B-26 G-25-MAs were the direct vision panel and the diagonal brace in the port windshield. The sickle shaped antenna, which was mounted offset to the port, close to the antenna mast, was relocated to the rear and centerline mounted in front of the vent boom for the wing tanks. The last model of the Marauder received an additional antenna behind the nose wheel bay. This antenna was slightly offset to port, so that the antenna cable did not touch the centerline-mounted teardrop-shaped radio compass covering.

All B-26 G-25-MAs were equipped with a static discharger on both wing tips, on the aileron, on the tail tip as well on both tips of the horizontal surfaces. The early examples of the B-26 G-25-MA had adopted the shark-tooth-shaped tab on the wing tip, but most aircraft from this block had this tab deleted on the production line.

The very last Marauder ever built first flew on 18 April 1945 from Martin's Middle River airfield. This B-26 G-25-MA had been built after a series of 32 TB-26 G-25-MA advanced trainers. At the controls of this bomber sat Chief Engineer William K. Ebel, who also took the first Marauder into the air on 25 November 1940. This last of the 5,266 Marauders built was the B-26 G-25-MA (44-68254), which employees of the Glenn L. Martin Company christened *Tail End Charlie – "30" –* . The – "30" – was a reference to the newspaperman's shorthand "– 30 –" that signified "end of the story."

A B-26 G-25-MA (44-68160) belonging to the 394th Bomb Group, 586th Bomb Squadron, 9th Air Force drops its load of two 2000 pound bombs over the marshalling yard at Ulm in Southern Germany in the closing days of World War II. The B-26 G-25-MA became the last version of the Marauder and was distinguished by having static discharger on both wing tips, the aileron, the tail tip as well on both tips of the horizontal surfaces, features that were not mounted on previous versions of the G-model. (USAF via Steve Birdsall)

A dedicated feature on the B-26 G-25-MA was the missing direct-vision panel and the missing diagonal brace in the port windshield. *Li'l Ass* had been assigned with the unit marking H9-J to the 394th Bomb Group, 586th Bomb Squadron. This brand new B-26 G-25-MA (44-68129) was based at A-74 Cambrais-Niergnies and already has the nickname painted on the armor plate but lacks any mission symbols. (Alain Pelletier)

B-26 G-25-MA Development

B-26 G-15-MA

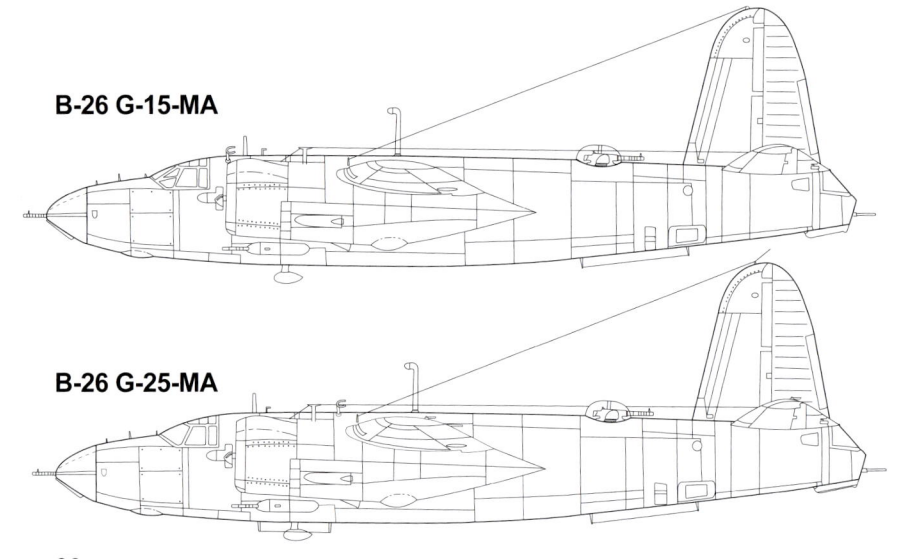

B-26 G-25-MA

B-26 G-25 MA

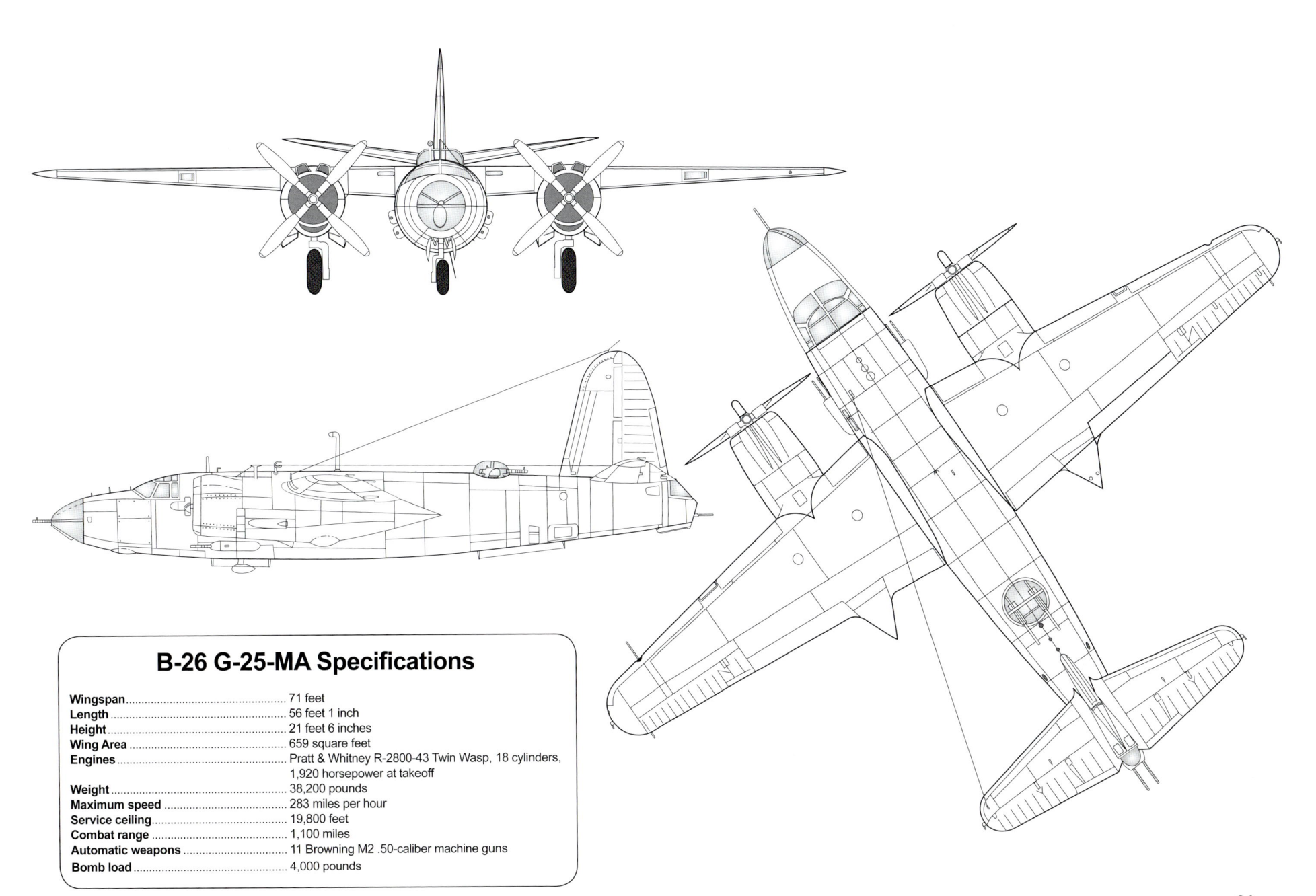

B-26 G-25-MA Specifications

Wingspan	71 feet
Length	56 feet 1 inch
Height	21 feet 6 inches
Wing Area	659 square feet
Engines	Pratt & Whitney R-2800-43 Twin Wasp, 18 cylinders, 1,920 horsepower at takeoff
Weight	38,200 pounds
Maximum speed	283 miles per hour
Service ceiling	19,800 feet
Combat range	1,100 miles
Automatic weapons	11 Browning M2 .50-caliber machine guns
Bomb load	4,000 pounds

A freshly arrived B-26 G-25-MA is in formation with a 320th Bomb Group, 444th Bomb Squadron B-26 C. Fighter escort is provided by a P-47 Thunderbolt belonging to the 86th Fighter Group with its distinctive white red striped tail. The B-26 G-25-MA lacks the distinctive shark mouth, which was the 444th Bomb Squadron marking. The last block of the Marauder had the sickle shaped antenna relocated to the rear, just in front of the periscope shaped vent-boom. (Dave Mickelson via Jack K. Havener)

The last Marauder ever built, B-26 G-25-MA (44-68254) first took to the air from Martin's Middle River airfield in Baltimore, Maryland, on 18 April 1945. The aircraft was later nicknamed *Tail End Charlie* – "30" –. (GLMMAM)

The Free French Air Force became the sole foreign air arm to be equipped with B-26 G-25-MA. Factory fresh examples of the last variant of the G-model had been delivered in early 1945 to the Frech Allies. This B-26 G-25-MA (44-68207) belonged to the 1ère Escadrille (1st Squadron) of the Groupe de Bombardement II/63 "Sénégal," as the unit badge below the cockpit denotes. The Battle Number 31 was applied in Green on the tail fin and white outlined. (Musée de l'Air)

The deleted direct vision panel as well the diagonal brace on the port windshield as well the relocated sickle shaped antenna are typical features for the B-26 G-25-MA, the last production batch of the Marauder. (GLMMAM)

XB-26 H

The XB-26 H was developed as a test bed to determinate the behavior of a bicycle-type landing gear on the future heavy jet-powered bombers that, in the closing weeks of World War II, were on the drawing boards of Boeing and Martin.

The testing began when one standard production B-26 G-25-MA (44-68221) was taken from the production line. Its forward gear was mounted in the aft section of the original nose gear well and the rear member was positioned in the aft section of the rear bomb bay. The wheels measured 17 x 20 inches and the forward gear was able to turn 30 degrees in either direction for steering. To prevent the unarmed XB-26 H from tipping over on the ground an outrigger gear was fitted in the engine nacelles.

The Bell M-6 A tail turret was replaced with a conical, redesigned tail with a fixed canopy taken over from the TB-26 G-25-MA advanced trainer. In addition, horizontal stabilization ribs were fitted on the surface skin of the fuselage.

Nicknamed *Middle River Stump Jumper*, the XB-26 H first flew on 4 May 1945. At the end of the factory test envelope the XB-26 H was dismantled and taken by road to Wright Field, where the USAAF trials started. The sole XB-26 H ever built returned to Baltimore after the Wright Field tests were complete. The bicycle-type landing gear – first tested on the XB-26 H – had been adopted on the Boeing B-47 Stratojet, which became the major Strategic Air Command (SAC) bomber.

The XB-26 H (44-68221) was nicknamed *Middle River Stump Jumper*. The test bed for a bicycle-type landing gear had additional horizontal stabilization ribs mounted on the fuselage. (GLMMAM)

A feature of the XB-26 H was the conical tail, which had been adopted from TB-26 G-25-MA advanced trainer. (GLMMAM)

The bicycle-type main landing gear had been added by an outrigger gear that was mounted in the engine nacelles. (GLMMAM)

TB-26 G-25-MA

The Middle River plant produced 32 advanced trainers under the designation TB-26 G-25-MA (Serial Numbers 44-68222 through 44-68253) in early spring 1945. As was the case with all Marauder trainers, defensive armament, external and internal armor protection, and all combat-related equipment were removed from the TB-26 G-25-MA airframe. The circular aperture for the Martin 250 CE turret was faired over. The TB-26 G-25-MA was delivered without the V-shaped brace in the Plexiglas nose. Its conical, redesigned tail had a fixed canopy from which the tail shell-case collector had been deleted. With the exception of the B-26 G-25-MA (Serial Number 44-68254) dubbed *Tail End Charlie – "30" –*, these TB-26 G-25-MAs were the last production examples of the Marauder. The final TB-26 G-25-MA came off the production line at Middle River on 30 March 1945.

JM-2 target tug

The JM-2 was a derivative of the TB-26 G advanced trainer, which in turn was based on the B-26 G-25-MA bomber. A total of 47 JM-2s (Bureau of Aeronautics numbers 90507 through 90521 and 91962 to 91993) were delivered to the U.S. Navy in March 1945. The Middle River plant made no new JM-2s for the Navy; all the JM-2s were in fact former TB-26 Gs initially manufactured for the Army Air Force. Most of these TB-26 G-25-MAs built for the Army were transferred directly to the Navy as JM-2s. The rest of the JM-2s were former TB-26 G-15-MAs and TB-26 G-20-MAs.

In contrast to the JM-1, which was based on the AT-23 B-MO (B-26 C), the JM-2 had no entrance door on the starboard tail. In contrast to the B-26 G-25-MA, the antenna mast located behind the nose wheel bay was deleted and replaced by a single pin-shaped antenna located behind the teardrop-shaped fairing for the radio compass. Like the JM-1, the JM-2 served as a target tug and most JM-2s were delivered in bright yellow. Over the course of their Navy service, however, the aircraft were painted dark blue. Navy JM-2s served much longer than did the Army Air Force B-26s. A number of JM-2s were still in service when the United States issued an order to paint the remaining aircraft in Gloss Sea Blue (ANA 623) on 2 January 1947.

This overall blue JM-2 (Bureau of Aeronautics Number 91972) once left the Middle River plant as an advanced trainer TB-26 G-25-MA. The TB-26 G-25-MA became the sole variant of the advanced trainer having a static discharger fitted on the wing leading edge as well the horizontal and vertical fin tips. This JM-2 belonged to the last block of Marauders built in March 1945. The JM-2 differed from the B-26 G-25-MA in having a conical tail with a fixed tail canopy in place of the Bell M-6A turret. The tail shell-case collector of the B-26 G-25-MA was deleted on the JM-2. No new JM-2 aircraft were built at the Middle River plant for the United States Navy; all JM-2s were in fact former TB-26 Gs ordered by the Army Air Corps. This particular JM-2 was repainted in the course of operation in Gloss Sea Blue (ANA 623), with an anti glare panel applied on the upper nose section in Non-specular Sea Blue (ANA 607). The national markings with the two red bars were introduced on 14 January 1947. (GLMMAM)

The JM-2 target tugs for the U.S. Navy were in fact TB-26 G advanced trainers that the Army Air Force turned over to the Navy. This JM-2 (Bureau of Aeronautics Number 91973) had been converted from a TB-26 G-25-MA. In contrast to the B-26 G-25-MA, no V-shaped brace was introduced in the Plexiglas nose. This particular JM-2 belonged to the VJ-4, a Navy utility squadron, as indicated by the marking on the nose. (GLMMAM)

Female employees of Glenn L. Martin factory in Middle River near Baltimore examine the conical tail section of JM-2s bound for the U.S. Navy in early 1945. All JM-2 target tugs were delivered unarmed and the electro-hydraulically powered Bell M-6 A tail turret of the B-26 G-25-MA bomber had been deleted in favor of a conical tail, while the upward hinged Plexiglas hood was retained. (Lockheed Martin)

Brand new JM-2 target tugs lined up at the Glenn L. Martin factory field in Middle River near Baltimore await delivery to the U.S. Navy. The unarmed JM-2 was based on the B-26 G-25-MA bomber. A total of 47 JM-2 (Bureau of Aeronautics numbers 90507 through 90521 and 91962 to 91993) were delivered to the United States Navy in March 1945. The JM-2 nearest camera has the Bureau of Aeronautics Number 90514. (GLMMAM)

This B-26 B-15-MA (41-31656) is *en route* to destroy German-held strong points in occupied France. The horizontal yellow stripe on the tail fin is the identification marking of the 386th Bomb Group. The two-letter code "AN" applied on the rear fuselage identifies this Marauder as belonging to the 553rd Bomb Squadron. This B-26 has the individual aircraft letter "H" applied on the tail. The crew christened this Marauder *Spare Parts*. The D-Day stripes have been partly overpainted on the wing and the rear fuselage. The Supreme Headquarters Allied Expeditionary Force (SHAEF) issued an order that these invasion stripes should be removed from the wing surfaces between 25 August and 10 September 1944. On 6 December 1944, the SHAEF ordered the removal of all invasion stripes from the aircraft. However, there were many former D-Day B-26s still carrying the invasion stripes on the fuselage in early 1945. This B-26 B-15-MA had left the assembly lines being painted in dark olive drab and arrived in Europe during June 1943. However, dark olive drab was prone to extreme fading, as this battered Marauder testifies. (John H. Meyers)

A three-ship formation of 320th Bomb Group, 441st Bomb Squadron Marauder performs a low-level flight. Nearest the camera is the B-26 G-5-MA (43-34252) *Sandra Lee* with the Battle Number 06, followed by the B-26 B-50-MA (42-96016) *Doris K* (Battle Number 04) and *Camellia*, a B-26 G-5-MA (43-34248) with the Battle Number 20. *Camellia* was reported as salvaged on 17 December 1944. (Joseph S. Kingsbury)

This brand new B-26 G-10-MA (43-34455) has freshly arrived from the United States. This Marauder was subsequently assigned to the 1st Pathfinder Squadron (Provisional) of the 9th Air Force and was lost near its home base A-72 Péronne in France on 29 January 1945. (Robert Foose)

Lieutenant John H. Meyers rests on the tail fin of the B-26 B-15-MA (41-31610). The yellow horizontal stripe on the tail fin is the distinctive identification marking for the 386th Bomb Group, which was based at A-60 Beaumont-sur-Oise in France. The Marauder has its 553rd Squadron marking AN-P applied on the rear fuselage. Its first crew choose the nickname *Hard Luck*. (John H. Meyers)

This B-26 G-5-MA (43-34389) belonging with the Battle Number 03 to the 320th Bomb Group, 441st Bomb Squadron suffered damage in the wing after a Messerschmitt Me 262 attack. The Marauder made it back to its home base at Y-9 Dijon-Longvic in France. (Joseph S. Kingsbury)

This B-26 C-20-MO (41-35117) was built by the Glenn L. Martin Nebraska Company at Omaha. The Marauder served with the 344th Bomb Group during their stateside training at Lakeland Air Force Base in Florida in November 1943. Large white digits were applied on training aircraft. (Jack K. Havener)

The four Rheinmetall-Borsig MK-108 30mm cannons mounted in the nose of the Messerschmitt Me 262 A-1a jet-powered fighter had a devastating effect. This B-26 G-5-MA (43-34389) of the 320th Bomb Group has been hit in the wing and the ailerons. The ailerons on all Marauders were fabric covered. (Joseph S. Kingsbury)

A B-26 B belonging to the 386th Bomb Group runs warm its Pratt & Whitney R-2800-43 Double Wasp powerplant on a snow covered hard stand. The Marauder's Browning M-2 0.50-caliber machine gun has been removed from the nose, as was common on B-26s operating in the closing months of World War II. The 386th Bomb Group unit operated from A-60 Beaumont-sur-Oise airbase in France during the harsh winter 1944-1945. It was about the time to say goodbye to the Marauder: the 386th Bomb Group switched in early 1945 from the B-26 to the Douglas A-26 Invader. (John H. Meyers)

Ground crews clean snow off of *La Paloma* at A-60 Beaumont-sur-Oise airbase prior a mission during the harsh winter 1944-1945. This B-26 G-1-MA (43-34210) was assigned to the 386th Bomb Group, 553rd Bomb Squadron. (John H. Meyers)

Captain John H. Meyers sits in the cockpit of the B-26 B-15-MA (41-31639) *Gamblers' Luck* that had been assigned with the unit marking RG-G to the 552nd Bomb Squadron of the A-60 Beaumont-sur-Oise based 386th Bomb Group. (John H. Meyers)

This 386th Bomb Group B-26 B takes part in a mission over occupied France. The invasion stripes, applied on all 9th Air Force aircraft that took part on D-Day, have here been overpainted. (John H. Meyers)

The lower gun pod has been removed from this B-26 belonging to the 320th Bomb Group. The upper gun pod remains, but the Browning M-2 0.50-caliber machine gun has been deleted. (Joseph S. Kingsbury)

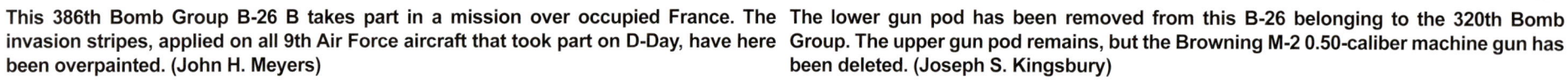

A formation of 443rd Squadron B-26s prepares for a mission from Y-9 Dijon-Longvic airdrome in France, the 320th Bomb Group's home base. Nicknamed Old Pop, the aircraft with the Battle Number 69 is a B-26 C-45-MO (42-107558). (Joseph S. Kingsbury)

Members of a crew pose in front of the B-26 B-50-MA (42-95990) Ol' Timer belonging with the Battle Number 18 to the 320th Bomb Group, 441st Bomb Squadron. Seen here without its two port gun pods, this B-26 survived the war. (Joseph S. Kingsbury)

Rat Poison rests at A-92 St. Trond airfield in Belgium, the home base of the 386th Bomb Group from early April 1945 until July 1945. The unit marking AN-S denotes that this B-26 B-15-MA (41-31606) belonged to the 553rd Bomb Squadron. *Rat Poison* had flown a total of 164 missions by February 1945, when the 386th BG flew its last mission on the Marauder an then converted to the Douglas A-26 Invader. There was only one other Marauder in the 386th Bomb Group that completed more missions than *Rat Poison*. This battered Marauder finished its 100th mission in early July 1944. *Rat Poison* was retained by the 386th Bomb Group and converted for use as a group transport. The mission markings as well the nickname were still applied on the veteran, when the B-26 B-15-MA served as a group transport in the closing weeks of World War II. (John H. Meyers)

This olive drab camouflaged B-26 served with the 344th Bomb Group during its stateside training at Lakeland Air Force Base, Florida, in November 1943. The nose of each of these training aircraft was painted in large white digits. (Jack K. Havener)

Miss Manchester was a B-26 B-50-MA (42-95884) that had been assigned with the Battle Number 14 to the 320th Bomb Group, 441st Bomb Squadron, 12th Air Force. This Marauder survived the war. (Joseph S. Kingsbury)

The Bell M-6 A tail turret had been introduced on the Army Air Corps Marauder for the first time on the B-26 G-1-MA. On the Bell M-6 A, the bulbous Plexiglas tail cap of the earlier Bell M-6 variant was replaced by a canvas covering. With the introduction of the Bell M-6 A, the tail was slightly redesigned: the rounded end skinning on the M-6 turret with a clear tail cap was replaced by straight linear skin on the tail. The first B-26 G-1-MA were assigned to the 9th Air Force during mid-August 1944. (John H. Meyers)

This B-26 B-55-MA (42-96128) crosses the English Channel *en route* to its target in occupied Europe. The Marauder had been assigned with the unit marking AN-N to the 386th Bomb Group, 553rd Bomb Squadron. The B-26 B-55-MA had been the last B-variant of the Marauder to be built at Martin's plant at Middle River in Baltimore. The first 101 B-26 B-55-MAs were delivered with camouflage consisting of dark olive drab with medium green on the upper surfaces to be used to soften the edges of tail planes and wings. The lower part of the airframe was painted in medium green. By end of January 1944 all B-26 B-55-MAs manufactured in Baltimore were delivered without any camouflage in bare aluminum silver. (John H. Meyers)

Captain John H. Meyers poses in front of an olive drab camouflaged B-26 Marauder at A-60 Beaumont-sur-Oise air base in France. The 386th Bomb Group was based at Beaumont-sur-Oise between 2 October 1944 and 9 April 1945. (John H. Meyers)

The 386th Bomb Group faced harsh winter conditions at its home base at A-60 Beaumont-sur-Oise during early 1945. The B-26 G-1-MA (43-34210) flew with the unit marking AN-V for the 553rd Bomb Squadron and carried the nickname *La Paloma*. (John H. Meyers)

This B-26 F-1-MA (42-96322) had been assigned with the Battle Number 07 to the 320th Bomb Group, 441st Bomb Squadron, which was part of the 12th Air Force in the Mediterranean Theater of Operations. This was one of the last of a total of 100 Marauder built under the contract AC-31733 in the F-1-MA block. There were only a few B-26 F-1-MA assigned to the 12th Air Force, the main part of this block went to the England based 9th Air Force. This Marauder survived the war. (Joseph S. Kingsbury)

B-26 Marauder belonging to the 320th Bomb Group, 12th Air Force performing with the help of the AN/APN-3 Shoran a bombing through overcast on a German railroad bridge during the closing weeks of World War II. The AN/APN-3 Shoran was a very accurate short range navigational system in blind bombing and had a range of 400 kilometers. Shoran became available for 12th Air Force Marauder units in spring 1945. (Joseph S. Kingsbury)

Captain John H. Meyers poses in front of the port Pratt & Whitney R-2800-43 Double Wasp powerplant of a B-26 Marauder. Captain John H. Meyers was assigned to the 386th Bomb Group, which was based before D-Day at Station 164 Great Dunmow in England. The surfaces of the engine cowling are missing of paint, which is a common sign of tear. (John H. Meyers)

This B-26 B-15-MA (41-31576), belonging to the 386th Bomb Group, 553rd Bomb Squadron, is crossing the English Channel some time before the Allied invasion at Normandy unfolded, as the lack of the black-white invasion stripes denotes. At this time, the group was based at Station 164 Great Dunmow in England. The Marauder had applied its unit marking AN-Z on the rear fuselage. The yellow horizontal stripe on the tail fin is the identification marking for the 386th Bomb Group. The B-26 had been christened by its crew *Dinah Might*. The Marauder was shot down by Luftwaffe fighters on 18 November 1944, when the 386th Bomb Group was on its 294th mission, striking a Wehrmacht storage depot at St. Wendel near Saarbrücken in South-Western Germany. (John H. Meyers)

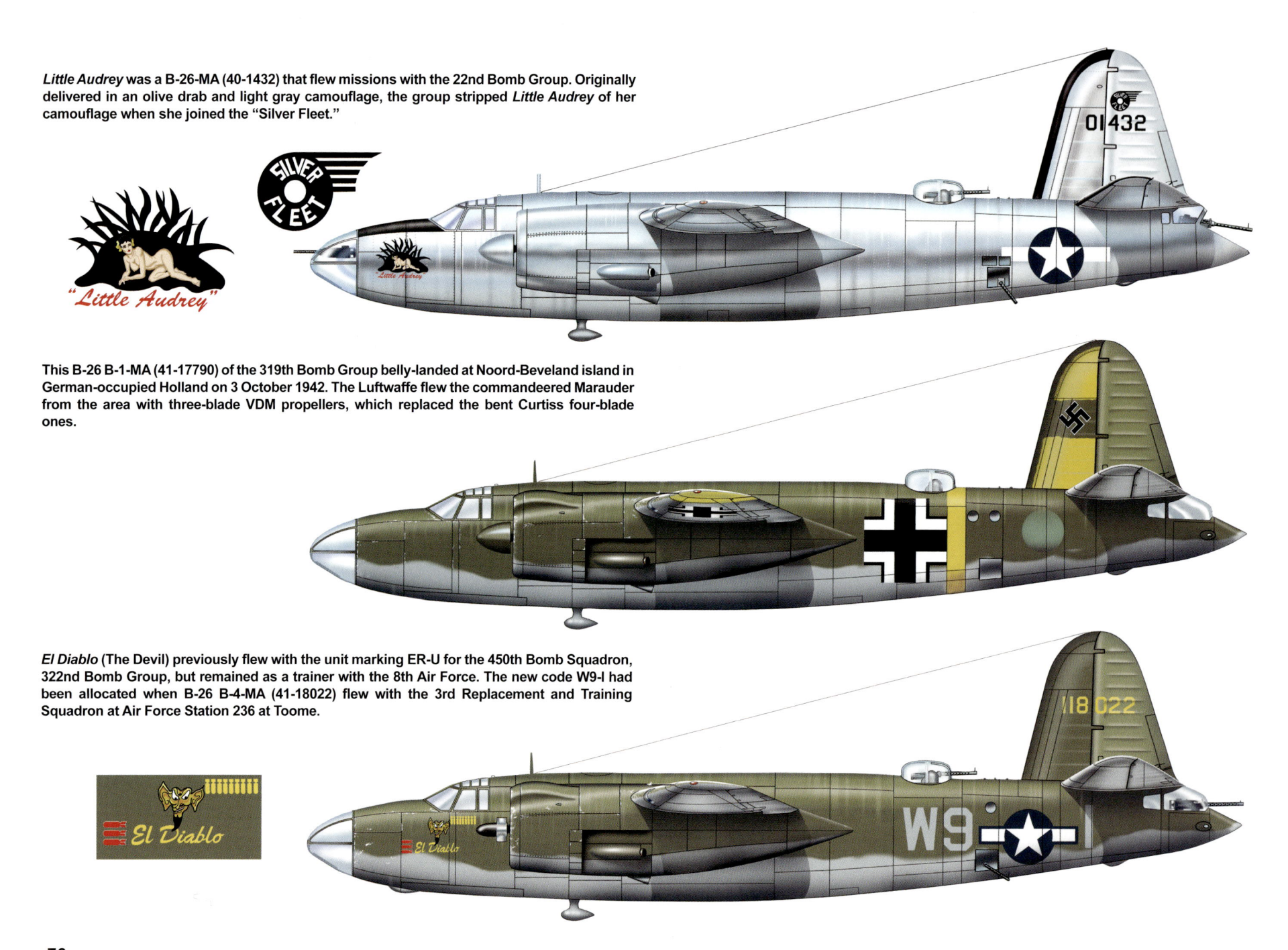

Little Audrey was a B-26-MA (40-1432) that flew missions with the 22nd Bomb Group. Originally delivered in an olive drab and light gray camouflage, the group stripped *Little Audrey* of her camouflage when she joined the "Silver Fleet."

This B-26 B-1-MA (41-17790) of the 319th Bomb Group belly-landed at Noord-Beveland island in German-occupied Holland on 3 October 1942. The Luftwaffe flew the commandeered Marauder from the area with three-blade VDM propellers, which replaced the bent Curtiss four-blade ones.

El Diablo (The Devil) previously flew with the unit marking ER-U for the 450th Bomb Squadron, 322nd Bomb Group, but remained as a trainer with the 8th Air Force. The new code W9-I had been allocated when B-26 B-4-MA (41-18022) flew with the 3rd Replacement and Training Squadron at Air Force Station 236 at Toome.

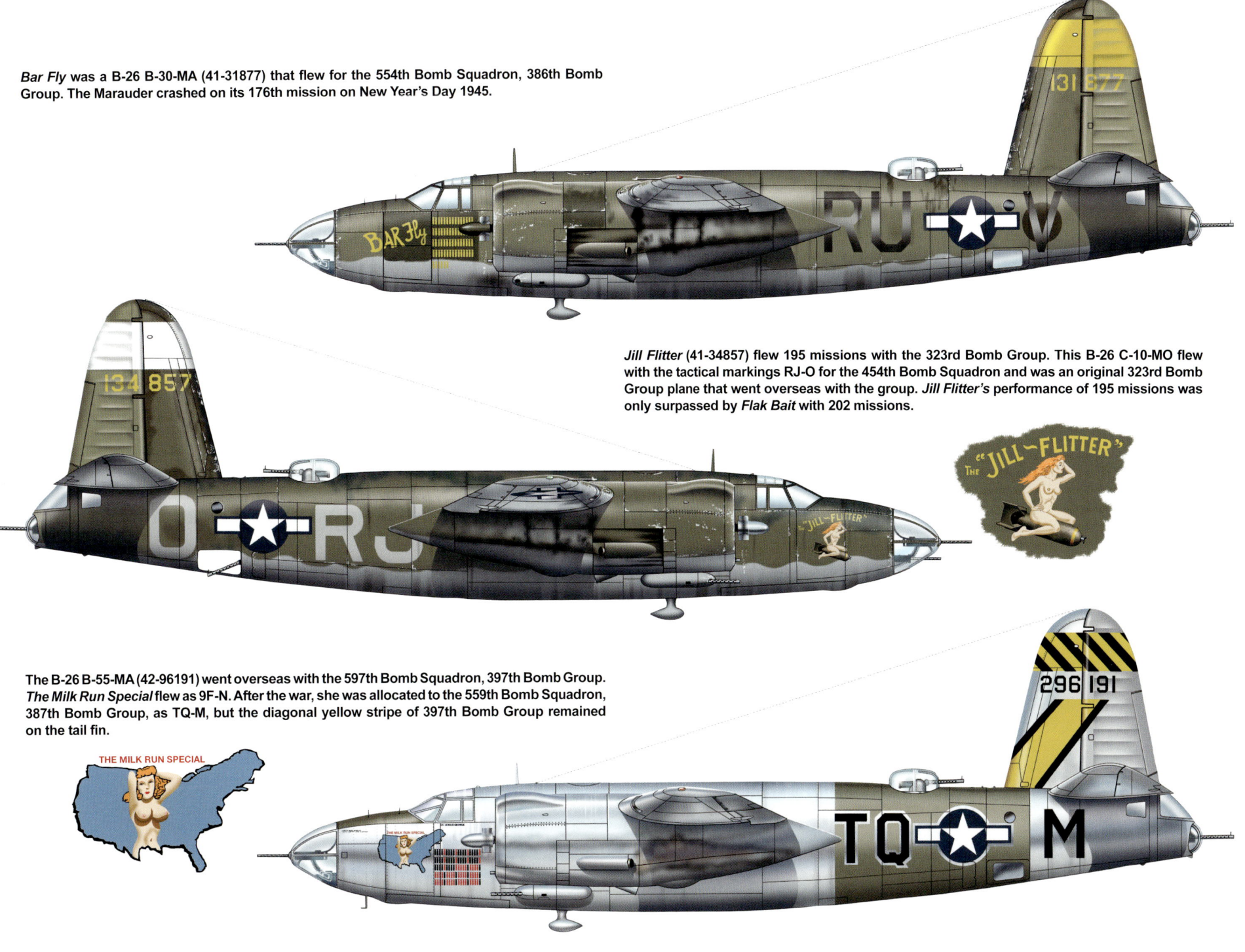

Bar Fly was a B-26 B-30-MA (41-31877) that flew for the 554th Bomb Squadron, 386th Bomb Group. The Marauder crashed on its 176th mission on New Year's Day 1945.

Jill Flitter (41-34857) flew 195 missions with the 323rd Bomb Group. This B-26 C-10-MO flew with the tactical markings RJ-O for the 454th Bomb Squadron and was an original 323rd Bomb Group plane that went overseas with the group. *Jill Flitter's* performance of 195 missions was only surpassed by *Flak Bait* with 202 missions.

The B-26 B-55-MA (42-96191) went overseas with the 597th Bomb Squadron, 397th Bomb Group. *The Milk Run Special* flew as 9F-N. After the war, she was allocated to the 559th Bomb Squadron, 387th Bomb Group, as TQ-M, but the diagonal yellow stripe of 397th Bomb Group remained on the tail fin.

77

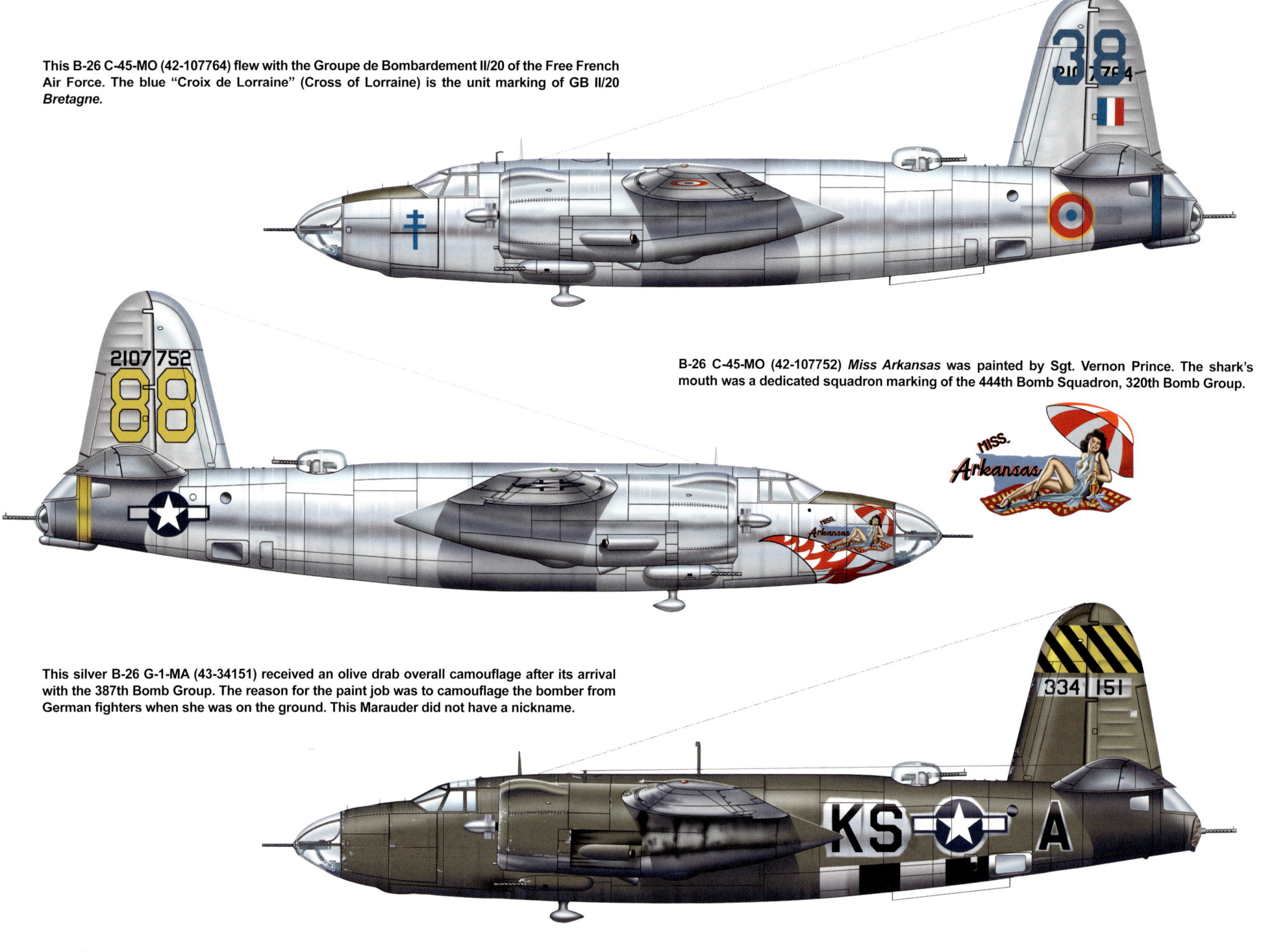

This B-26 C-45-MO (42-107764) flew with the Groupe de Bombardement II/20 of the Free French Air Force. The blue "Croix de Lorraine" (Cross of Lorraine) is the unit marking of GB II/20 *Bretagne*.

B-26 C-45-MO (42-107752) *Miss Arkansas* was painted by Sgt. Vernon Prince. The shark's mouth was a dedicated squadron marking of the 444th Bomb Squadron, 320th Bomb Group.

This silver B-26 G-1-MA (43-34151) received an olive drab overall camouflage after its arrival with the 387th Bomb Group. The reason for the paint job was to camouflage the bomber from German fighters when she was on the ground. This Marauder did not have a nickname.

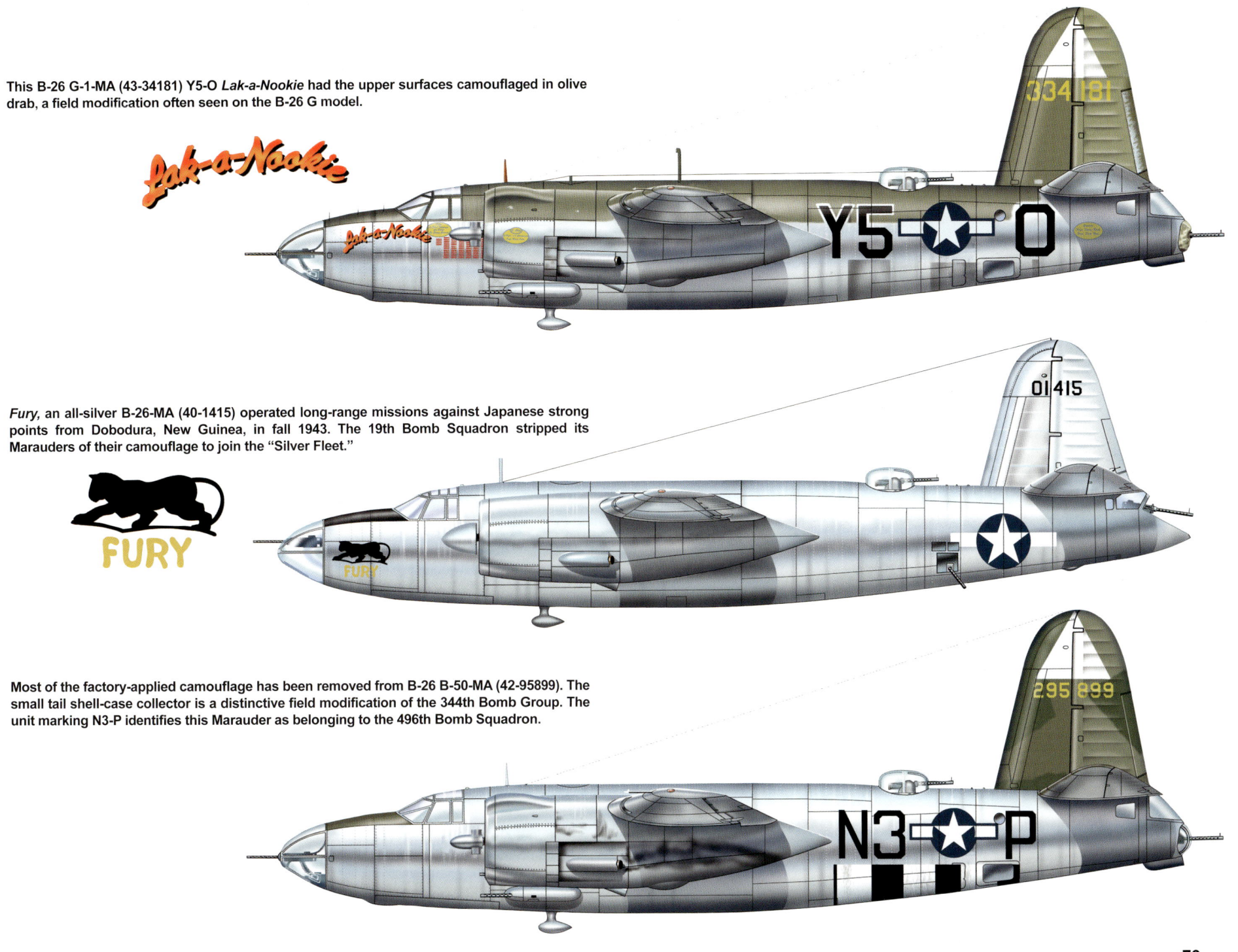

This B-26 G-1-MA (43-34181) Y5-O *Lak-a-Nookie* had the upper surfaces camouflaged in olive drab, a field modification often seen on the B-26 G model.

Fury, an all-silver B-26-MA (40-1415) operated long-range missions against Japanese strong points from Dobodura, New Guinea, in fall 1943. The 19th Bomb Squadron stripped its Marauders of their camouflage to join the "Silver Fleet."

Most of the factory-applied camouflage has been removed from B-26 B-50-MA (42-95899). The small tail shell-case collector is a distinctive field modification of the 344th Bomb Group. The unit marking N3-P identifies this Marauder as belonging to the 496th Bomb Squadron.

The very last Marauder ever built is rolled out: B-26 G-25-MA (44-68254) *Tail End Charlie – "30"* – first flew on 18 April 1945 from Martin's Middle River airfield in Baltimore, Maryland. This B-26 G-25-MA had been built after a series of 32 TB-26 G-25-MA advanced trainers. Like most late production B-26 Gs, this aircraft received camouflage on the upper surface of the wing and fuselage at the factory. At the controls of *Tail End Charlie – "30"* – sat Chief Engineer William K. Ebel, who had also taken the very first Marauder into the air on 25 November 1940. The employees of the Glenn L. Martin Company christened this last of the 5,266 Marauders *Tail End Charlie – "30"* –. The – *"30"* – was an allusion to the newspaperman's shorthand "– 30 –" that signified "end of story." (Steve Birdsall)